PLASTIC CANVAS

HEAVENLY CREATIONS ™

Editor	JUDY CROW
Assistant Editors	SHIRLEY PATRICK
	SHIRLEY BROWN
Book Design	GREG SMITH
Production Artist	DEBBY KEEL
Photography Supervisor	SCOTT CAMPBELL
Photographer	ANDY J. BURNFIELD
Photo Department Assistants	MARTHA COQUAT
	CRYSTAL KEY
Chief Executive Officer	JOHN ROBINSON
Publishing Director	DAVID MCKEE
Editorial Director	VIVIAN ROTHE
Editorial Manager	CONNIE ELLISON
Publishing Services Manager	ANGE VAN ARMAN
Customer Service	(800) 449-0440
Pattern Services	(903) 636-5140

Credits

Sincerest thanks to all the designers,
manufacturers and other professionals
whose dedication has made this book possible.

Special thanks to
Quebecor Printing Book Group, Kingsport, Tenn.

Library of Congress Cataloging-in-Publication Data
ISBN: 1-57367-127-4
First Printing: 2003
Library of Congress Catalog Card Number: 2002112822
Published and Distributed by
The Needlecraft Shop, Big Sandy, TX 75755
Printed in the United States of America.

Visit us at
NeedlecraftShop.com

Dear Friends,

Each of us is inspired in different ways. For a crafter, that inspiration can come from skeins of yarn, needles and plastic canvas. Without the inspiration of a great pattern, all these items are in vain.

Most of us are not designers, although we may change the color in a pattern to match our decor. We depend on the creativity of others. Our greatest pleasure comes from stitching and constructing each piece into something we've only seen in a photo.

We also delight in using our handiwork to bring warm hospitality into our homes, to make fun treasures for our children as well as to create great handmade gifts for family and friends that make a special occasion even more unforgettable.

The selection of projects in this book is meant to spread radiant sunshine all year long. You'll surely be inspired to Share The Love with these heavenly crosses or to Count Your Blessings by giving a beautiful Prayer Book to a friend. Reflections of Faith may be displayed with the Holy City Tissue Cover or you may select a guardian angel from the Band of Angels. Whichever design you choose to make, it's sure to be divine.

As an inspired crafter, our halo really shines when showered with praise and thanks for our efforts and a job well done. If your want your halo to shine, begin stitching these heavenly projects today!

Judy

Table of
Contents

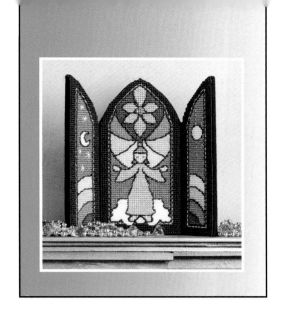

Share the
Love

"All that we are we will pass on to our children—our loves, our hopes, our dreams, our character. Therefore, let your thoughts be planted in rich soil and let your actions stand tall in a child's eyes. Just as fruit does not fall far from the tree, children do not stray far from their heroes."

Author Unknown

Chapter

Chrismon Ornaments

Designed by Janna Britton

SIZES
Crown is 2⅞" x 4" [7.3cm x 10.2cm]; Jerusalem Cross is 4¼" x 4¼" [10.8cm x 10.8cm]; CHI-RHO is 3½" x 5½" [8.9cm x 14cm]; Manger is 3½" x 4¾" [8.9cm x 12.1cm]; Lamp is 3" x 5¼" [7.6cm x 13.3cm]; Fish is 3½" x 6¼" [8.9cm x 15.9cm]; Flame is 3⅞" x 5¼" [9.8cm x 13.3cm], not including hangers

SKILL LEVEL
Average

MATERIALS FOR ALL
- Two Sheets of 7-mesh QuickCount® Plastic Canvas by Uniek Inc.
- One Plastic Canvas QuickShape™ 5" [12.7cm] Star by Uniek Inc.
- One Plastic Canvas QuickShape™ 3" [7.6cm] Circle by Uniek Inc.
- Cabochons by The Beadery:
  1 Pear 25 x 18mm Crystal #006
  2 Pear 18 x 13mm Crystal #006
  2 Navette 18 x 8mm Crystal #006
  3 Round 7mm Topaz #23
  6 Round 6mm Topaz #23
- Two white 9" x 12" [22.9cm x 30.5cm] sheets of felt
- Craft glue or glue gun
- Needloft® Metallic Craft Cord by Uniek Inc. (for amounts see Color Key)
- ¼" [6mm] metallic ribbon (for amount see Color Key)
- ⅛" [3mm] Metallic Ribbon by Kreinik Metallics (for amount see Color Key)
- Metallic Cord by Kreinik Metallics (for amount see Color Key)
- Needloft® Plastic Canvas Yarn by Uniek Inc. or worsted yarn (for amount see Color Key)

CUTTING INSTRUCTIONS
A: For Crown, cut one according to graph.
B: For Jerusalem Cross, cut one according to graph.
C: For CHI-RHO "P", cut one according to graph.
D: For CHI-RHO "X", cut one according to graph.
E: For Manger, cut one according to graph.
F: For Manger Legs, cut one according to graph.
G: For Baby's Head, cut one from circle according to graph.
H: For Lamp, cut one according to graph.
I: For Fish Body, cut one according to graph.
J: For Fish Tail, cut one from star according to graph.
K: For Flame Piece #1, cut one according to graph.
L: For Flame Piece #2, cut one according to graph.

STITCHING INSTRUCTIONS
1: Using colors and stitches indicated, work pieces according to graphs; with matching and indicated colors and as shown in photo, overcast edges of pieces.

2: Using metallic cord and ¼" ribbon and embroidery stitches indicated, embroider detail on H and K pieces as indicated on graphs.

3: For CHI-RHO, glue wrong side of "X" to right side of "P" (see photo). For Manger, glue right side of G to wrong side of E and wrong side of E to right side of F as shown. For Fish, glue unworked area of J to wrong side of I. For Flame, glue wrong side of L to right side of K as indicated.

NOTE: Using each Ornament as a pattern, cut one each from felt ⅛" [3mm] smaller at all edges for backings.

4: Glue corresponding felt backing to wrong side of each Ornament. Glue cabochons to A as indicated. Hang as desired.

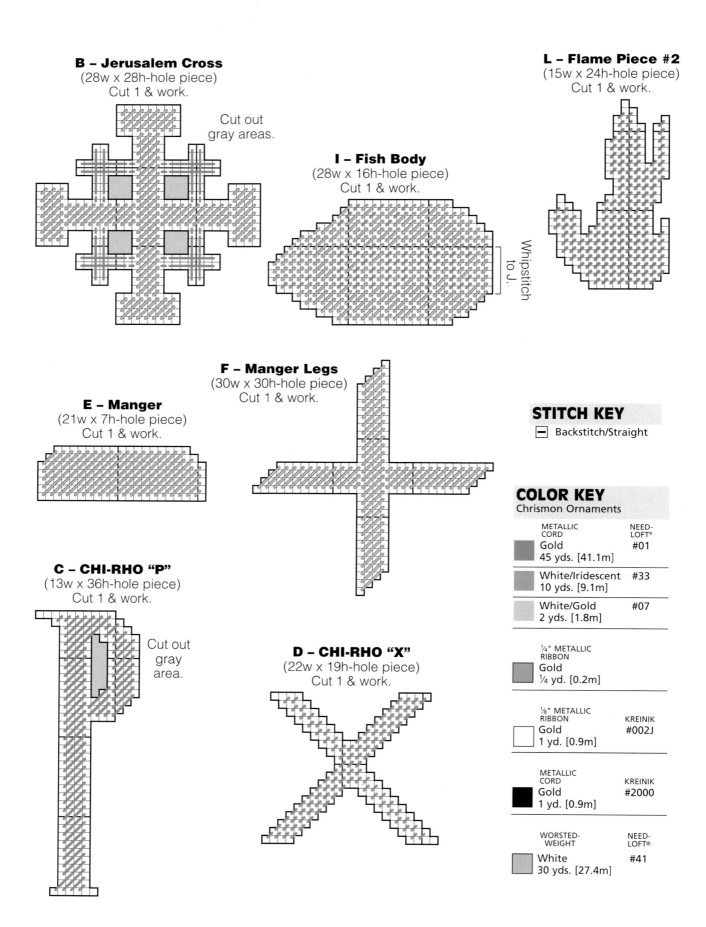

B – Jerusalem Cross
(28w x 28h-hole piece)
Cut 1 & work.

Cut out
gray areas.

I – Fish Body
(28w x 16h-hole piece)
Cut 1 & work.

Whipstitch
to J.

L – Flame Piece #2
(15w x 24h-hole piece)
Cut 1 & work.

F – Manger Legs
(30w x 30h-hole piece)
Cut 1 & work.

E – Manger
(21w x 7h-hole piece)
Cut 1 & work.

STITCH KEY

⊟ Backstitch/Straight

COLOR KEY
Chrismon Ornaments

	METALLIC CORD	NEED-LOFT®
	Gold 45 yds. [41.1m]	#01
	White/Iridescent 10 yds. [9.1m]	#33
	White/Gold 2 yds. [1.8m]	#07

	¼" METALLIC RIBBON	
	Gold ¼ yd. [0.2m]	

	⅛" METALLIC RIBBON	KREINIK
	Gold 1 yd. [0.9m]	#002J

	METALLIC CORD	KREINIK
	Gold 1 yd. [0.9m]	#2000

	WORSTED-WEIGHT	NEED-LOFT®
	White 30 yds. [27.4m]	#41

C – CHI-RHO "P"
(13w x 36h-hole piece)
Cut 1 & work.

Cut out
gray
area.

D – CHI-RHO "X"
(22w x 19h-hole piece)
Cut 1 & work.

K – Flame Piece #1
(25w x 34h-hole piece)
Cut 1 & work.

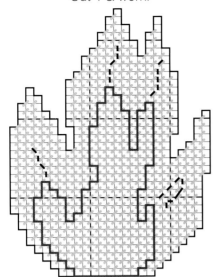

PLACEMENT KEY
☐ Flame Piece #2 /Flame Piece #1

G – Baby's Head
(3" circle) Cut 1 & work, leaving uncoded area unworked.

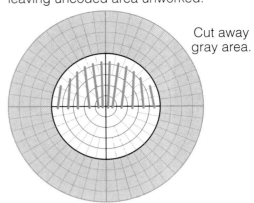

Cut away gray area.

H – The Lamp
(34w x 19h-hole piece)
Cut 1 & work.

Overcast with 1/8" gold ribbon between arrows.

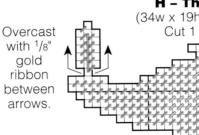

Cut out gray area.

J – Fish Tail
(star shape) Cut 1 & work, leaving uncoded area unworked.

Cut away gray area.

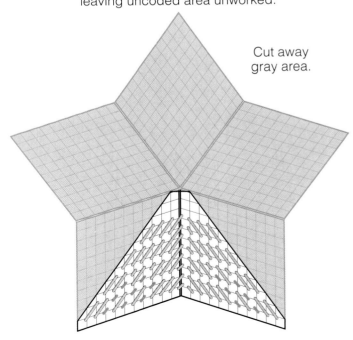

A – Crown
(26w x 19h-hole piece)
Cut 1 & work.

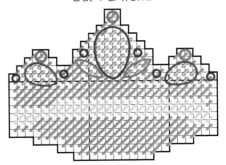

CABOCHONS
☐ 25 x 18mm Crystal
☐ 18 x 13mm Crystal
☐ 18 x 8mm Crystal
☐ 7mm Topaz
☐ 6mm Topaz

Faith, Hope & Love Bookmarks

Designed by Mary T. Cosgrove

SIZE
Each Bookmark is 2½" x 9" [6.4cm x 22.9cm], not including tassel

SKILL LEVEL
Average

MATERIALS FOR ALL
- One Sheet of 7-mesh QuickCount® Plastic Canvas by Uniek Inc.
- Craft glue or glue gun
- Needloft® Plastic Canvas Yarn by Uniek Inc. or worsted yarn (for amounts see Color Key)

CUTTING INSTRUCTIONS
A: For "Faith", cut one according to graph.
B: For "Hope", cut one according to graph.
C: For "Love", cut one according to graph.

STITCHING INSTRUCTIONS
1: Using colors and stitches indicated, work A-C pieces according to graphs. With gold for letters and outer edges and with matching colors, overcast cutouts and outer edges of pieces.

2: Using colors indicated and straight stitch, embroider detail on A and B pieces as indicated on graphs.

NOTE: Cut twelve 9" [22.9cm] lengths of gold.

3: For each tassel (make 3), holding four strands together as one, fold in half and tie into a knot close to fold; center and glue fold to wrong side of bottom edge of one Bookmark (see photo).

COLOR KEY
"Faith" Bookmark

	WORSTED-WEIGHT	NEED-LOFT®
☐	Eggshell 10 yds. [9.1m]	#39
	Gold 10 yds. [9.1m]	#17
	Purple 8 yds. [7.3m]	#46

STITCH KEY
⊟ Straight

A – "Faith"
(17w x 60h-hole piece)
Cut 1 & work, filling in uncoded areas using eggshell & continental stitch.

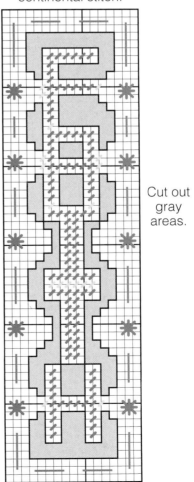

Cut out gray areas.

B – "Hope"
(17w x 60h-hole piece)
Cut 1 & work, filling
in uncoded areas
using eggshell &
continental stitch.

C – "Love"
(17w x 60h-hole piece)
Cut 1 & work, filling
in uncoded areas
using eggshell &
continental stitch.

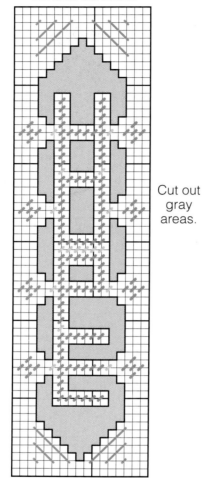

Cut out
gray
areas.

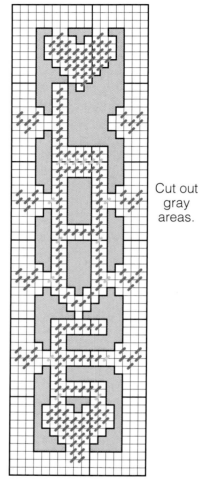

Cut out
gray
areas.

COLOR KEY
"Hope" Bookmark

	WORSTED-WEIGHT	NEED-LOFT®
	Eggshell 10 yds. [9.1m]	#39
	Gold 10 yds. [9.1m]	#17
	Holly 6 yds. [5.5m]	#27

COLOR KEY
"Love" Bookmark

	WORSTED-WEIGHT	NEED-LOFT®
	Eggshell 8 yds. [7.3m]	#39
	Gold 8 yds. [7.3m]	#17
	Burgundy 6 yds. [5.5m]	#03

STITCH KEY
− Straight

Inspirational Fridgies

Designed by Eunice Asberry

SIZE
Each is about 1¼" x 2" [3.2cm x 5.1cm]

SKILL LEVEL
Average

MATERIALS FOR ALL
- ¼ sheet of 10-mesh plastic canvas
- 3" [7.6cm] piece of magnetic strip
- Craft glue or glue gun
- Six-strand Metallic Embroidery Floss Art. 317 by DMC® (for amount see Color Key on page 16)
- Sport-weight yarn (for amounts see Color Key)

CUTTING INSTRUCTIONS
A: For Bible, cut one according to graph.

B: For Cross, cut one according to graph.

C: For Angel, cut one according to graph.

STITCHING INSTRUCTIONS
1: Using colors and stitches indicated, work pieces according to graphs; with indicated and matching colors and as shown in photo, overcast edges of pieces.

2: Using 3 strands floss and yarn (Separate into individual plies if desired.) and embroidery stitches indicated, embroider detail on pieces as indicated on graphs.

3: Cut magnetic strip into three desired lengths; glue one to wrong side of each magnet.

A – Bible
(14w x 20h-hole piece)
Cut 1 & work.

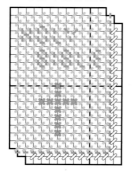

B – Cross
(14w x 20h-hole piece)
Cut 1 & work, filling in
uncoded areas using
white & continental stitch.

C – Angel
(12w x 19h-hole piece)
Cut 1 & work.

Overcast
with yellow.

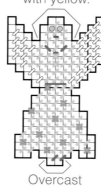

Overcast
with yellow.

COLOR KEY
Inspirational Fridgies

	METALLIC FLOSS	DMC®
	Gold 4 yds. [3.7m]	#284

	SPORT-WEIGHT	
	White 6 yds. [5.5m]	
	Royal 4 yds. [3.7m]	
	Green 1 yd. [0.9m]	
	Light Yellow ½ yd. [0.5m]	
	Purple ½ yd. [0.5m]	
	Yellow ½ yd. [0.5m]	
	Flesh Tone ¼ yd. [0.2m]	
	Pink ¼ yd. [0.2m]	

STITCH KEY
– Backstitch/Straight
● French Knot

Layered Cross

Designed by Kathy Wirth

SIZE
8¼" x 10" [21cm x 25.4cm]

SKILL LEVEL
Challenging

MATERIALS
- Three Sheets of Black 7-mesh QuickCount® Plastic Canvas by Uniek Inc.
- Six Ruby 7mm Round Acrylic Cabochons by The Beadery
- Black 9" x 12" [22.9cm x 30.5cm] sheet of felt
- Craft glue of glue gun
- Metallic Plastic Canvas 10 Yarn by Rainbow Gallery (for amounts see Color Key)

CUTTING INSTRUCTIONS
A: For Base, cut two according to graph.
B: For Layer #1, cut two according to graph.
C: For Layer #2, cut twelve 9w x 9h-holes.
D: For Layer #3, cut twelve 7w x 7h-holes.
E: For Layer #4, cut twelve 5w x 5h-holes.
F: For Layer #5, cut twelve 3w x 3h-holes.

STITCHING INSTRUCTIONS
NOTE: Using B as a pattern, cut one from felt ⅛" [3mm] smaller at all edges.

1: Using colors and stitches indicated, work A and B pieces according to graphs.

2: For each stack (make 6), using colors and stitches indicated, position two of each C-F pieces at each indicated area on right side of B and work through all thicknesses as one.

3: Glue felt to wrong side of Cross; glue cabochons to Layer 5 as indicated on graphs. Hang or display as desired.

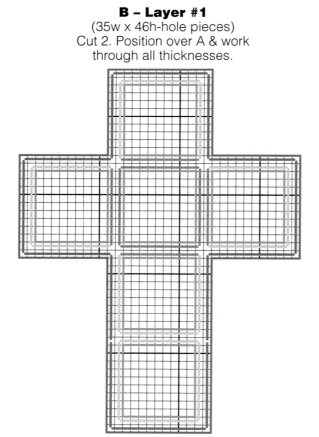

B – Layer #1
(35w x 46h-hole pieces)
Cut 2. Position over A & work
through all thicknesses.

COLOR KEY
Layered Cross

	METALLIC PC10 YARN	RAINBOW GALLERY®
Gold 10 yds. [9.1m]		#PM51
Silver 10 yds. [9.1m]		#PM52
Red 4 yds. [3.7m]		#PM55

PLACEMENT KEY
☐ B/A Placement
☐ C/B Placement
☐ D/C Placement
☐ E/D Placement
☐ F/E Placement

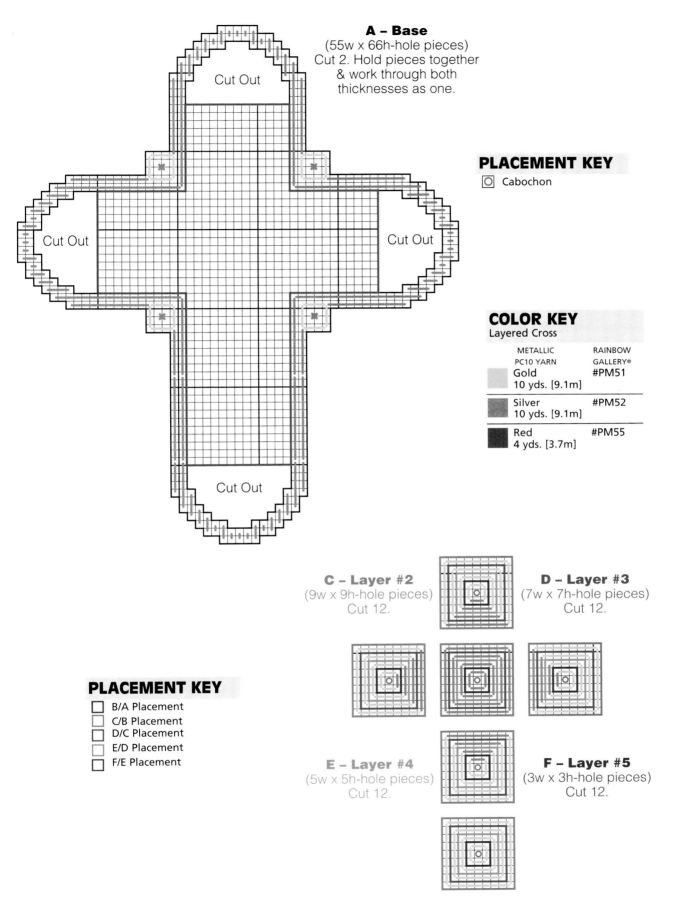

A – Base
(55w x 66h-hole pieces)
Cut 2. Hold pieces together
& work through both
thicknesses as one.

Cut Out

Cut Out

Cut Out

Cut Out

PLACEMENT KEY

⊡ Cabochon

COLOR KEY
Layered Cross

	METALLIC PC10 YARN	RAINBOW GALLERY®
Gold 10 yds. [9.1m]		#PM51
Silver 10 yds. [9.1m]		#PM52
Red 4 yds. [3.7m]		#PM55

C – Layer #2
(9w x 9h-hole pieces)
Cut 12.

D – Layer #3
(7w x 7h-hole pieces)
Cut 12.

E – Layer #4
(5w x 5h-hole pieces)
Cut 12.

F – Layer #5
(3w x 3h-hole pieces)
Cut 12.

PLACEMENT KEY

☐ B/A Placement
☐ C/B Placement
☐ D/C Placement
☐ E/D Placement
☐ F/E Placement

Let Us Pray

Designed by Carol Krob

SIZE
Bookmark is 2" x 13" [5.1cm x 33cm],
including Cross

SKILL LEVEL
Challenging

MATERIALS
- ½ sheet of 14-mesh plastic canvas
- One Package each Mill Hill Victoria Gold
  Glass Seed Beads #22011 and White Glass
  Seed Beads #20479 by Gay Bowles Sales Inc.
- Two gold 6mm round cabochons
- Beading needle and thread
- Craft glue or glue gun
- ¹⁄₁₆" [2mm] Metallic Ribbon by Kreinik
  Metallics (for amounts see Color Key)

CUTTING INSTRUCTIONS
  A: For Bookmark Front and Backing, cut two
(one for Front and one for Backing) according to
graph.
  B: For Cross, cut two according to graph.

STITCHING INSTRUCTIONS

NOTE: Backing A is not worked.

1: Omitting beads, using colors and stitches indicated, work Front A according to graph.

2: Using gold and straight stitch, embroider detail on Front A as indicated on graph. Using beading needle and thread, attach beads to Front A and B pieces as indicated and according to Bead Attachment Illustration. Glue cabochons to B pieces as indicated.

NOTE: Cut one 8" [20.3cm] length of gold.

3: Insert one end of ribbon from front to back through one ◆ hole on Front A and from back to front through remaining ◆ hole.

4: Holding Backing A to wrong side of Front A, with gold, whipstitch together. Whipstitch B pieces wrong sides together, holding knotted end of ribbon between B pieces and whipstitching around ribbon (see photo).

Bead Attachment Illustration

COLOR KEY
Let Us Pray

	METALLIC RIBBON	KREINIK
	Pearl 10 yds. [9.1m]	#032
	Gold 10 yds. [9.1m]	#002HL

ATTACHMENT KEY
☐ Victorian Gold Seed Beads
☐ White Seed Beads

PLACEMENT KEY
☐ Cabochon

STITCH KEY
– Straight

A – Bookmark Front and Backing
(26w x 114h-hole pieces)
Cut 2; work 1 for Front & leave 1 unworked for Backing.

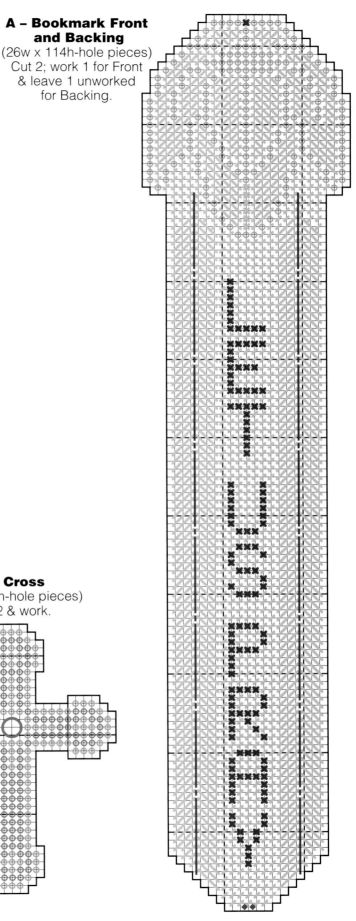

B – Cross
(26w x 34h-hole pieces)
Cut 2 & work.

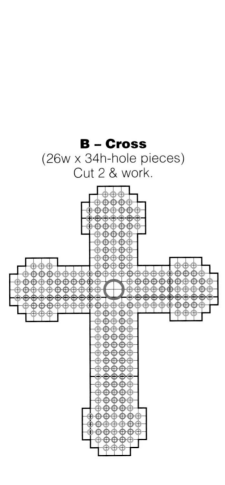

Rejoice Cross

Designed by Nancy Billetdeaux

SIZE
11" x 13½" [27.9cm x 34.3cm], not including wreath and flowers

SKILL LEVEL
Average

MATERIALS
- Two Sheets of 7-mesh QuickCount® Plastic Canvas by Uniek Inc.
- Scrap Piece of 10-mesh QuickCount® Plastic Canvas by Uniek Inc.
- 3" [7.6cm] grapevine wreath
- Seven white ½" [13mm] silk rose buds
- Two ¾" x 1½" [1.9cm x 3.8cm] artificial green leaves
- One 12" x 18" [30.5cm x 45.7cm] sheet of white felt
- Craft glue or glue gun
- Needloft® Metallic Craft Cord by Uniek Inc.

(for amount see Color Key).
- Needloft® Plastic Canvas Yarn by Uniek Inc. or worsted yarn (for amounts see Color Key)

CUTTING INSTRUCTIONS
A: For Front, cut one from 7-mesh according to graph.

B: For Back, cut one from 7-mesh according to graph.

C: For Sign, cut one from 10-mesh 26w x 5h-holes.

STITCHING INSTRUCTIONS
NOTE: Separate yarn into 2 plys for stitching C.

1: Using colors and stitches indicated, work A-C pieces according to graphs; with white for C and with matching colors, overcast edges of A-C pieces.

NOTE: Using B as a pattern, cut one from felt ⅛" [3mm] smaller at all edges.

2: Glue felt to wrong side of B. Center and glue wrong side of A to right side of B. Glue rose buds, leaves and Sign to wreath and wreath to right side of A as shown in photo. Hang as desired.

A – Front
(64w x 64h-hole piece)
Cut 1 from 7-mesh & work.

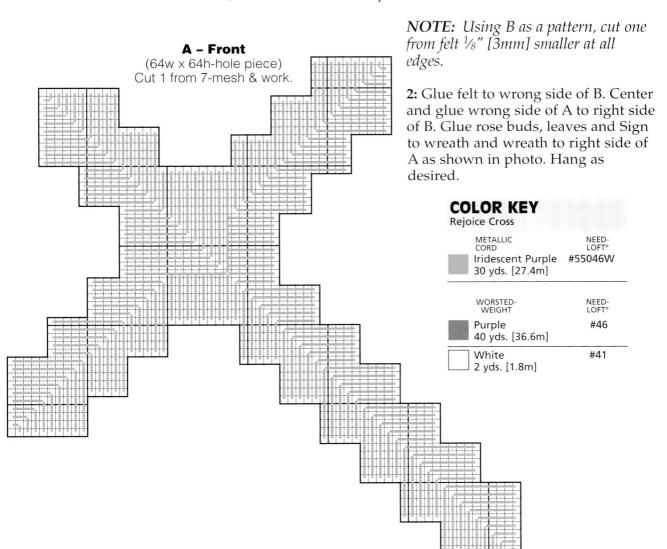

COLOR KEY
Rejoice Cross

METALLIC CORD		NEEDLOFT®
Iridescent Purple 30 yds. [27.4m]		#55046W

WORSTED-WEIGHT		NEEDLOFT®
Purple 40 yds. [36.6m]		#46
White 2 yds. [1.8m]		#41

B – Back
(68w x 68h-hole piece)
Cut 1 from 7-mesh & work.

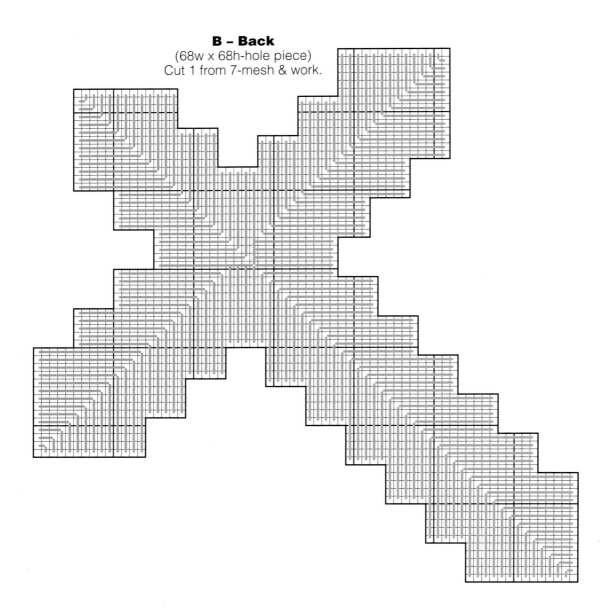

COLOR KEY
Rejoice Cross

	METALLIC CORD	NEED-LOFT®
	Iridescent Purple 30 yds. [27.4m]	#55046W

	WORSTED-WEIGHT	NEED-LOFT®
	Purple 40 yds. [36.6m]	#46
	White 2 yds. [1.8m]	#41

C – Sign
(26w x 5h-hole piece)
Cut 1 from 10-mesh & work.

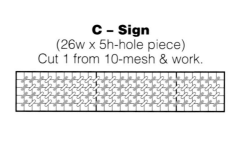

Wire Crosses

Designed by Lee Lindeman

SIZES
Cross #1 is 3¾" x 5⅝" [9.5cm x 14.3cm];
Cross #2 is 4⅛" x 6" [10.5cm x 15.2cm];
Cross #3 is 4¾" x 5⅞" [12.1cm x 15cm];
Cross #4 is 2⅝" x 4" [6.7cm x 10.2cm];
Cross #5 is 3¼" x 4¾" [8.3cm x 12.1cm];
Cross #6 is 2⅛" x 3½" [5.4cm x 8.9cm]

SKILL LEVEL
Average

MATERIALS
- ½ sheet of 7-mesh plastic canvas for each Cross
- Four gold ⅜" [10mm] coin charms (for Cross #3)
- 1¾ yds. [1.6m] gold 18-gauge wire (for Crosses #2, #3, #4, #5 and #6)
- Craft glue or glue gun
- Needloft® Metallic Craft Cord by Uniek Inc. (for amounts see individual Color Keys).
- Needloft® Plastic Canvas Yarn by Uniek Inc. (for amounts, see individual Color Keys)

CUTTING INSTRUCTIONS
A: For Cross #1, cut two according to graph.
B: For Cross #2, cut two according to graph.
C: For Cross #3, cut two according to graph.
D: For Cross #4, cut two according to graph.
E: For Cross #5, cut two according to graph.
F: For Cross #6, cut two according to graph.

STITCHING INSTRUCTIONS

1: Using colors and stitches indicated, work pieces according to graph of choice.

NOTE: Cut sixteen 7" [17.8cm] lengths of silver metallic cord. For each spiral (make 16) tightly coil one length between fingers, gluing as you coil.

2: For Cross #1, with white, whipstitch A pieces wrong sides together. Glue spirals to Cross as shown in photo or as desired.

NOTE: Cut twelve 1½" [3.8cm] lengths of wire.

3: For Cross #2, position and glue wire lengths to wrong side of one B as shown. With flesh tone, whipstitch B pieces wrong sides together, stitching around wire.

NOTE: Cut four 1½" [3.8cm] lengths of wire. Insert one wire through each charm; bend one end of wire into a circle to hold charm (see photo).

4: For Cross #3, position and glue wire lengths to wrong side of one C as shown. With red, whipstitch C pieces wrong sides together, stitching around wire.

NOTE: Cut four 1½" [3.8cm] and four 2" [5.1cm] lengths of wire. Bend each wire into a semicircle (see photo).

5: For Cross #4, position and glue wire lengths to wrong side of one D as shown. With purple, whipstitch D pieces wrong sides together, stitching around wire.

NOTE: Cut eight 1½" [3.8cm] lengths of wire. Bend one end of each wire into a loop (see photo).

6: For Cross #5, position and glue wire lengths to wrong side of one E as shown. With tangerine, whipstitch E pieces wrong sides together, stitching around wire.

NOTE: Cut one 4" [10.2cm] and one 6¼" [15.9cm] lengths of wire. Bend and shape each wire into a circle.

7: For Cross #6, position and glue wire circles to wrong side of one F as shown. With bright blue, whipstitch F pieces wrong sides together, stitching around wire.

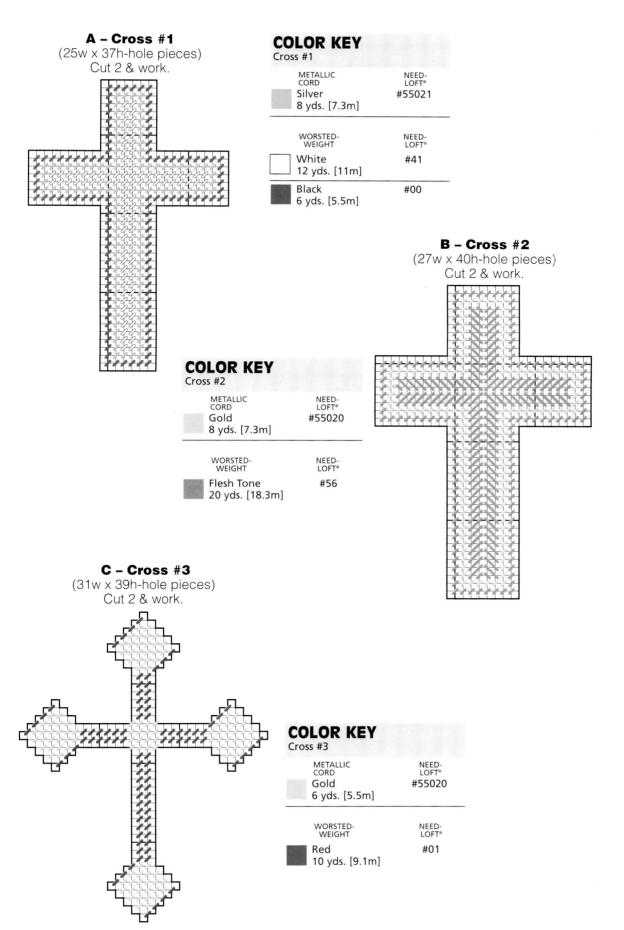

A – Cross #1
(25w x 37h-hole pieces)
Cut 2 & work.

COLOR KEY
Cross #1

METALLIC CORD	NEED-LOFT®
Silver 8 yds. [7.3m]	#55021

WORSTED-WEIGHT	NEED-LOFT®
White 12 yds. [11m]	#41
Black 6 yds. [5.5m]	#00

B – Cross #2
(27w x 40h-hole pieces)
Cut 2 & work.

COLOR KEY
Cross #2

METALLIC CORD	NEED-LOFT®
Gold 8 yds. [7.3m]	#55020

WORSTED-WEIGHT	NEED-LOFT®
Flesh Tone 20 yds. [18.3m]	#56

C – Cross #3
(31w x 39h-hole pieces)
Cut 2 & work.

COLOR KEY
Cross #3

METALLIC CORD	NEED-LOFT®
Gold 6 yds. [5.5m]	#55020

WORSTED-WEIGHT	NEED-LOFT®
Red 10 yds. [9.1m]	#01

D – Cross #4
(17w x 26h-hole pieces)
Cut 2 & work.

E – Cross #5
(22w x 31h-hole pieces)
Cut 2 & work.

F – Cross #6
(14w x 23h-hole pieces)
Cut 2 & work.

COLOR KEY
Cross #4

	METALLIC CORD	NEED-LOFT®
	Gold 5 yds. [4.6m]	#55020

	WORSTED-WEIGHT	NEED-LOFT®
	Purple 10 yds. [9.1m]	#46

COLOR KEY
Cross #5

	METALLIC CORD	NEED-LOFT®
	Gold 6 yds. [5.5m]	#55020

	WORSTED-WEIGHT	NEED-LOFT®
	Tangerine 8 yds. [7.3m]	#11

COLOR KEY
Cross #6

	METALLIC CORD	NEED-LOFT®
	Gold 4 yds. [3.7m]	#55020

	WORSTED-WEIGHT	NEED-LOFT®
	Bright Blue 8 yds. [7.3m]	#60

Star of David Ornament

Designed by Joan Green

SIZE
4½" x 5¼" [11.4cm x 13.3cm], not including hanger

SKILL LEVEL
Average

MATERIALS
- ½ sheet of 7-mesh plastic canvas
- 12 Assorted-color 4mm Faceted Gemstones from The Beadery
- Craft glue or glue gun
- Metallic Plastic Canvas Yarn by Rainbow Gallery (for amounts see Color Key)

CUTTING INSTRUCTIONS
A: For Star of David Piece #1, cut one according to graph.

B: For Star of David Piece #2, cut one according to graph.

STITCHING INSTRUCTIONS
1: Using colors and stitches indicated, work pieces according to graphs; omitting cut edges on A, with royal blue, overcast edges.

2: Interlock pieces as shown in photo. With royal blue, whipstitch cut edges of A together as indicated on graph. Glue pieces at areas where they cross to secure; glue gemstones to Ornament as indicated. Hang or display as desired.

A – Star of David Piece #1
(30w x 27h-hole piece)
Cut 1 & work, leaving royal blue stitches unworked.

Carefully cut through bars at dotted line.

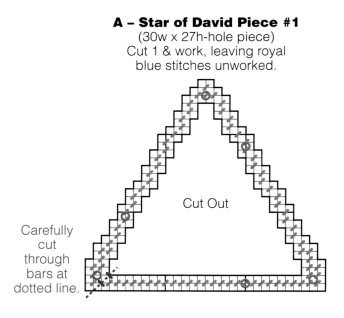

Cut Out

COLOR KEY
Star of David Ornament

	METALLIC CORD	RAINBOW GALLERY®
	Royal Blue 8 yds. [7.3m]	#PC06
	Silver 4 yds. [3.7m]	#PC02

B – Star of David Piece #2
(30w x 27h-hole piece)
Cut 1 & work.

Cut Out

PLACEMENT KEY
▢ Gemstone

30 Heavenly Creations

Cross Shaped Box

Designed by Joan Green

SIZE
6" x 8" x 1¾" tall [15.2cm x 20.3cm x 4.4cm]

SKILL LEVEL
Average

MATERIALS
- 2 sheets of 7-mesh plastic canvas
- 1 white 9mm pearl cabochon
- 12 pearl 4mm beads
- 20 gold 3mm beads
- Beading needle and white thread
- One 9" x 12" [22.9cm x 30.5cm] sheet of gray felt
- Craft glue or glue gun
- Metallic Plastic Canvas Yarn by Rainbow Gallery (for amounts see Color Key).
- Worsted-weight or plastic canvas yarn (for amount see Color Key)

CUTTING INSTRUCTIONS
A: For Lid Top, cut one according to graph.
B: For Lid Side #1, cut ten 13w x 5h-holes (no graph).
C: For Lid Side #2, cut two 26w x 5h-holes (no graph).
D: For Box Side #1, cut ten 12w x 9h-holes (no graph).
E: For Box Side #2, cut two 25w x 9h-holes (no graph).
F: For Box Bottom, cut one according to graph.

STITCHING INSTRUCTIONS
NOTE: F is not worked.

1: Using colors and stitches indicated, work A according to graph; work B-E pieces according to corresponding Stitch Pattern Guides.

2: Using gold and embroidery stitches indicated, embroider detail on A as indicated on graph. Using beading needle and thread, attach beads to A as indicated; glue cabochon to A as indicated.

NOTE: For Bottom backing, using F as a pattern, cut one from felt ⅛" [3mm] smaller at all edges.

3: For Box Lid, with gold, whipstitch A-C pieces together as indicated; overcast unfinished edges. For Box, with purple yarn, whipstitch D-F pieces together as indicated; overcast unfinished edges. Glue backing to bottom of Box.

Lid Side Stitch Pattern Guide

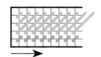

Continue established pattern across each entire piece.

Box Side Stitch Pattern Guide

Continue established pattern across each entire piece.

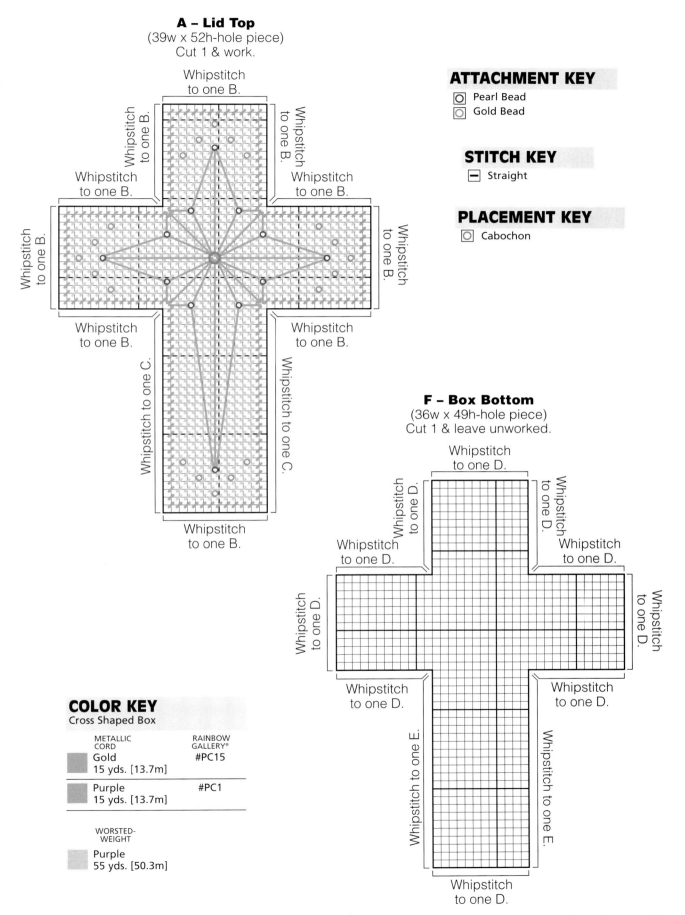

A – Lid Top
(39w x 52h-hole piece)
Cut 1 & work.

Whipstitch to one B.

Whipstitch to one B.

Whipstitch to one B.

Whipstitch to one B.

Whipstitch to one B.

Whipstitch to one B.

Whipstitch to one B.

Whipstitch to one B.

Whipstitch to one B.

Whipstitch to one C.

Whipstitch to one C.

Whipstitch to one B.

ATTACHMENT KEY

◎ Pearl Bead
◎ Gold Bead

STITCH KEY

⊟ Straight

PLACEMENT KEY

◻ Cabochon

F – Box Bottom
(36w x 49h-hole piece)
Cut 1 & leave unworked.

Whipstitch to one D.

Whipstitch to one D.

Whipstitch to one D.

Whipstitch to one D.

Whipstitch to one D.

Whipstitch to one D.

Whipstitch to one D.

Whipstitch to one D.

Whipstitch to one E.

Whipstitch to one E.

Whipstitch to one D.

COLOR KEY
Cross Shaped Box

	METALLIC CORD	RAINBOW GALLERY®
▨	Gold 15 yds. [13.7m]	#PC15
▨	Purple 15 yds. [13.7m]	#PC1

	WORSTED-WEIGHT	
▨	Purple 55 yds. [50.3m]	

Bible Cover

Designed by Barbara Ivie

SIZE
Covers a 2" x 8½" x 11¼" [5.1cm x 21.6cm x 28.6cm] Bible

SKILL LEVEL
Average

MATERIALS
• Three sheets of 7-mesh plastic canvas
• Eighty-one white 6mm pearl beads

C – Spine
(17w x 79h-hole piece)
Cut 1 & work.

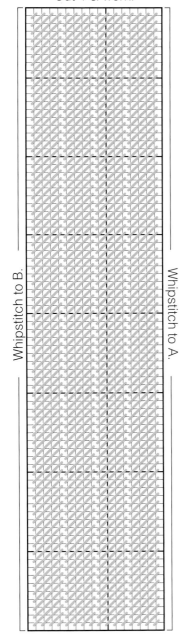

Whipstitch to B.

Whipstitch to A.

• Beading needle and white thread
• Metallic cord (for amount see Color Key)
• Worsted-weight or plastic canvas yarn
 (for amounts see Color Key)

CUTTING INSTRUCTIONS
   A: For Front, cut one 61w x 79h-holes.
   B: For Back, cut one 61w x 79h-holes.
   C: For Spine, cut one 17w x 79h-holes.
   D: For Inside Flaps, cut two 19w x 79h-holes (no graph).

STITCHING INSTRUCTIONS
NOTE: D pieces are not worked.

1: Using colors and stitches indicated, work pieces according to graphs.

2: Using sewing needle and thread, sew pearls to A and B pieces as indicated on graphs.

3: With royal blue, whipstitch A-D pieces together as indicated and according to Cover Assembly Illustration; overcast unfinished edges of A-C pieces.

COLOR KEY
Bible Cover

	METALLIC CORD	
▨	Gold	50 yds. [45.7m]

	WORSTED-WEIGHT	
▨	Royal Blue	3 oz. [85.1g]
☐	White	15 yds. [13.7m]

ATTACHMENT KEY
◻ Pearl Bead

Cover Assembly Illustration

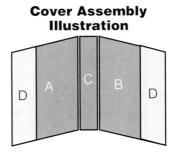

A – Front
(61w x 79h-hole piece)
Cut 1 & work.

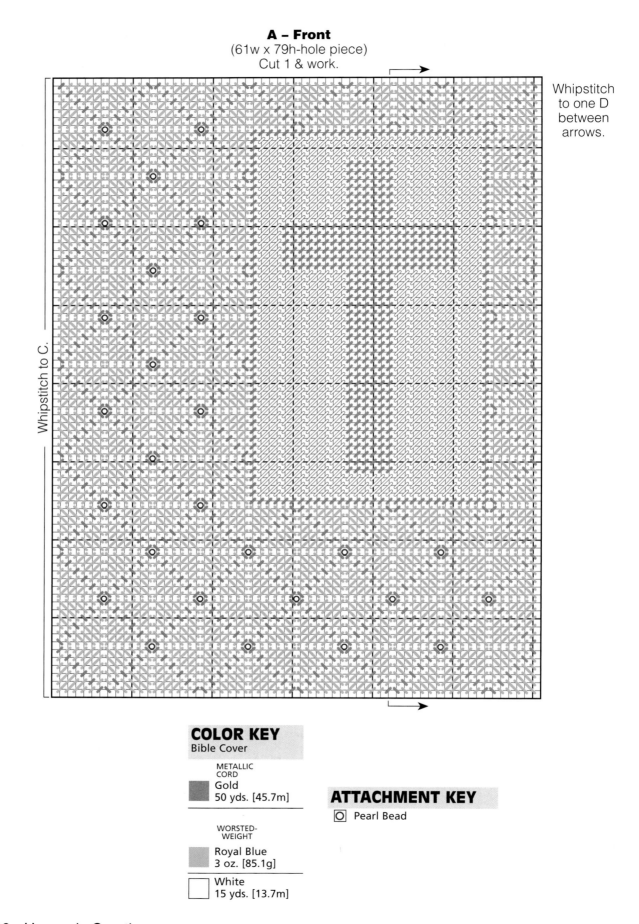

Whipstitch
to one D
between
arrows.

Whipstitch to C.

B – Back
(61w x 79h-hole piece)
Cut 1 & work.

Whipstitch
to one D
between
arrows.

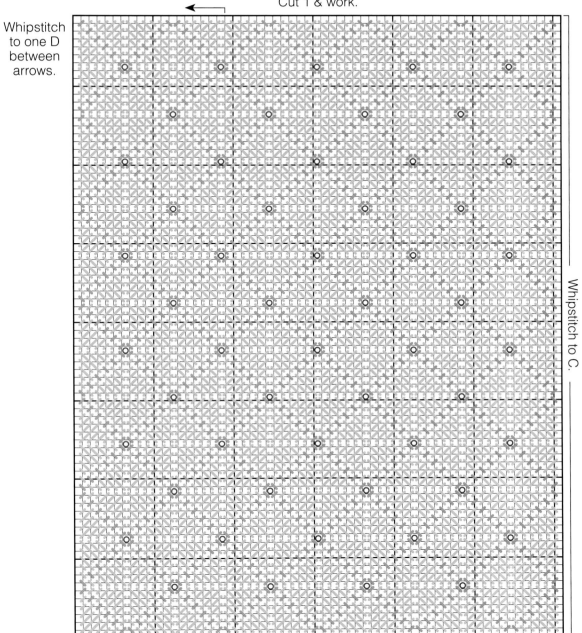

Whipstitch to C.

Count Your *Blessings*

Count your blessings
  instead of your crosses;
Count your gains
  instead of your losses.
Count your joys
  instead of your woes;
Count your friends
  instead of your foes.
Count your health
  instead of your wealth;
Love your neighbor
  as much as yourself.

Author Unknown

Chapter Two

Waves and Shells

Designed by Janna Britton

SIZES
Tissue Box Cover loosely covers a boutique-style tissue box; Stationery Holder is 2½" x 10⅛" x 3¼" tall [6.4cm x 25.7cm x 8.3cm], not including shells; Frame is 11⅝" x 11¾" [29.5cm x 29.8cm], not including shells

SKILL LEVEL
Average

MATERIALS FOR ALL
- Four Sheets of 7-mesh QuickCount® Plastic Canvas by Uniek Inc.
- One Sheet of 10-mesh QuickCount® Plastic Canvas by Uniek Inc.
- Thirteen assorted size and shape shells
- Velcro® closure (optional)
- Craft glue or glue gun
- No. 3 Pearl Cotton (coton perlé) Art. 115 by DMC® (for amounts see Color Key)
- Six-strand Embroidery Floss Art. 117 by DMC® (for amounts see Color Key)
- Needloft® Plastic Canvas Yarn by Uniek Inc. or worsted yarn (for amounts see Color Key)

CUTTING INSTRUCTIONS
A: For Tissue Cover Top, cut one from 7-mesh according to graph.

B: For Tissue Cover Sides, cut four from 7-mesh 34w x 38h-holes.

C: For Tissue Cover Optional Bottom and Flap, cut one from 7-mesh 34w x 34h-holes for Bottom and one from 7-mesh 34w x 12h-holes for Flap (no graphs).

D: For Stationery Holder Front, cut one from 7-mesh according to graph.

E: For Stationery Holder Back, cut one from 7-mesh 67w x 21h-holes (no graph).

F: For Stationery Holder Sides #1 and #2, cut one each from 7-mesh according to graphs.

G: For Stationery Holder Bottom, cut one from 7-mesh 67w x 15h-holes (no graph).

H: For Frame Front, cut one from 7-mesh according to graph.

I: For Frame Back, cut one from 10-count 99w x 110h-holes.

J: For Frame Corner Pieces, cut four from 7-mesh 14w x 14h-holes.

STITCHING INSTRUCTIONS
NOTE: C, E and G pieces are not worked.

1: Using colors and stitches indicated, work A, B, D, F, H-J pieces according to graphs; with baby blue for Tissue Cover Top cutout and sail blue for Frame Front cutout and with matching colors, overcast edges of H and J pieces and cutouts on A and H pieces.

2: Using pearl cotton and backstitch, embroider detail on B pieces as indicated on graph. Holding three strands of each color embroidery floss together as one and using embroidery stitches indicated, embroider detail on I as indicated.

3: With matching colors as shown in photo, whipstitch A and B pieces wrong sides together, forming Cover. For Optional Bottom, with baby blue, whipstitch C pieces together and to one Cover Side according to Optional Bottom Assembly Illustration on page 43. Separate Velcro® closure; glue one side to Flap and one side to inside of corresponding Cover Side. Overcast unfinished edges of Cover. Glue four shells to Cover as shown or as desired.

4: With sail blue, whipstitch D-G pieces together as indicated, forming Stationery Holder; overcast edges of Front and Side pieces. Glue three shells to Holder as shown or as desired.

5: Center Frame Back in cutout of Frame Front and glue to wrong side of H; glue wrong side of J pieces to right side of Frame Front as indicated. Glue remaining shells to Frame Front as shown or as desired.

A – Tissue Cover Top
(34w x 34h-hole piece)
Cut 1 from 7-mesh & work, filling in uncoded
areas using flesh tone & continental stitch.

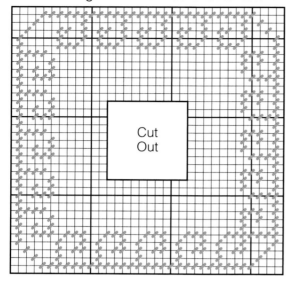

Cut
Out

B – Tissue Cover Side
(34w x 38h-hole pieces)
Cut 4 from 7-mesh & work, filling in uncoded
area using flesh tone & continental stitch.

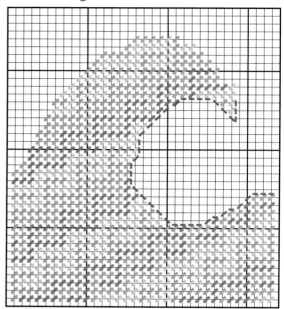

STITCH KEY
- Backstitch/Straight
● French Knot

D – Stationery Holder Front
(67w x 15h-hole piece) Cut 1 from 7-mesh & work.

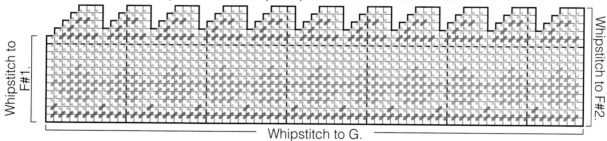

Whipstitch to F#1.

Whipstitch to F#2.

Whipstitch to G.

F – Stationery
Holder Side #1
(15w x 21h-hole piece)
Cut 1 from 7-mesh & work.

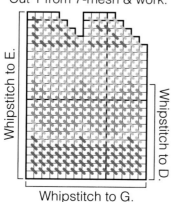

Whipstitch to E.

Whipstitch to D.

Whipstitch to G.

J – Frame
Corner Pieces
(14w x 14h-hole pieces)
Cut 4 from 7-mesh & work.

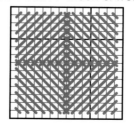

F – Stationery
Holder Side #2
(15w x 21h-hole piece)
Cut 1 from 7-mesh & work.

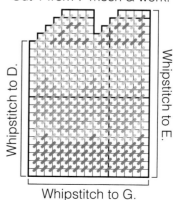

Whipstitch to D.

Whipstitch to E.

Whipstitch to G.

H – Frame Front

(76w x 77h-hole piece) Cut 1 from 7-mesh & work,
leaving uncoded areas unworked.

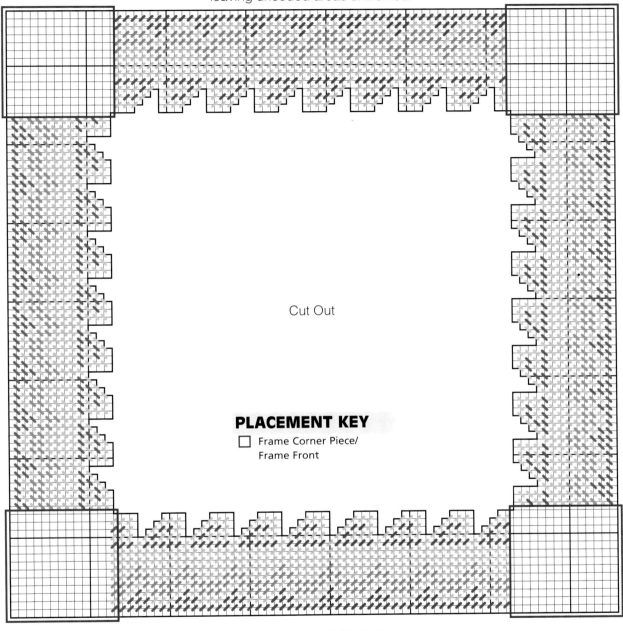

Cut Out

PLACEMENT KEY

☐ Frame Corner Piece/
Frame Front

COLOR KEY
Waves and Shells

	3 STRANDS FLOSS EACH	DMC®
■	Med. Jade/Sky Blue 9 yds. [8.2m] each	#562/#519

	NO. 3 PEARL COTTON	DMC®
	Cream 3 oz. [85.1g]	#712
■	Ultra Vy. Lt. Blue 3 yds. [2.7m]	#828

	WORSTED-WEIGHT	NEED-LOFT®
☐	Flesh Tone 55 yds. [50.3m]	#56
	Baby Blue 50 yds. [45.7m]	#36
■	Sail Blue 35 yds. [32m]	#35
	Moss 30 yds. [27.4m]	#25
	Mermaid 28 yds. [25.6m]	#53

Optional Tissue Cover Bottom Assembly Illustration

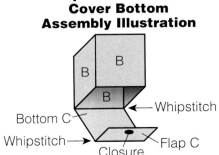

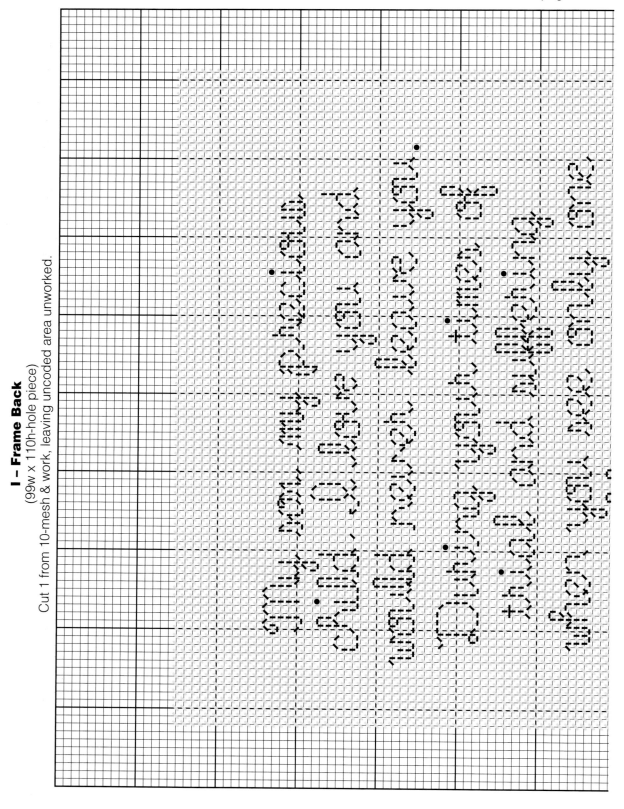

I – Frame Back
(99w x 110h-hole piece)
Cut 1 from 10-mesh & work, leaving uncoded area unworked.

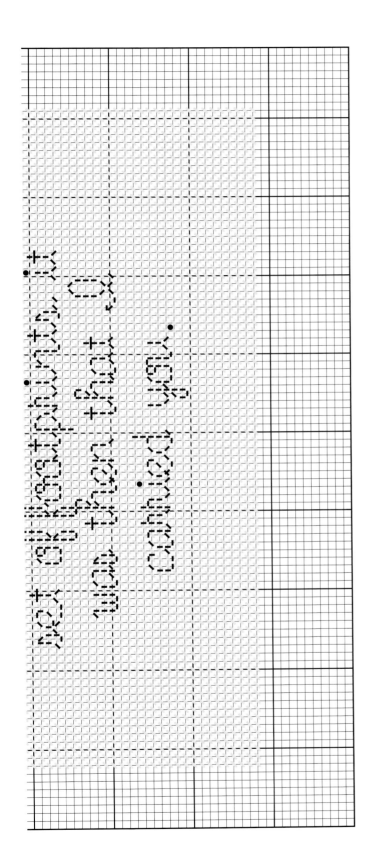

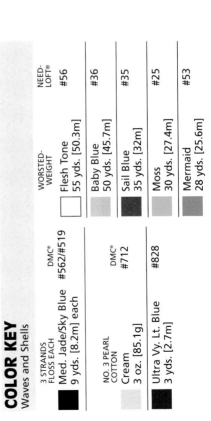

STITCH KEY

	Backstitch/Straight
●	French Knot

COLOR KEY
Waves and Shells

			WORSTED-WEIGHT	NEED-LOFT®
			Flesh Tone 55 yds. [50.3m]	#56
			Baby Blue 50 yds. [45.7m]	#36
			Sail Blue 35 yds. [32m]	#35
			Moss 30 yds. [27.4m]	#25
			Mermaid 28 yds. [25.6m]	#53

	3 STRANDS FLOSS EACH	DMC®
	Med. Jade/Sky Blue 9 yds. [8.2m] each	#562/#519

	NO. 3 PEARL COTTON	DMC®
	Cream 3 oz. [85.1g]	#712
	Ultra Vy. Lt. Blue 3 yds. [2.7m]	#828

Sunday School
Bible Bookmarks

Designed by Janelle Giese

SIZE
Each is 3" x 9⅛" [7.6cm x 23.1cm]

SKILL LEVEL
Average

MATERIALS FOR ALL
- ½ Sheet of white 7-mesh QuickCount® Plastic Canvas by Uniek Inc.
- No. 5 Pearl Cotton (coton perlé) Art. 116 by DMC® (for amount see Color Key)
- Needloft® Plastic Canvas Yarn by Uniek Inc. or worsted yarn (for amounts see Color Key)

CUTTING INSTRUCTIONS
A: For Kitty, cut one according to graph.
B: For Puppy, cut one according to graph.

STITCHING INSTRUCTIONS
1: Using colors and stitches indicated, work pieces according to graphs; with matching colors as shown in photo, overcast edges of worked areas only.

2: Using pearl cotton and yarn (Separate into individual plies if desired.) and embroidery stitches indicated, embroider detail on pieces as indicated on graphs.

B – Puppy
(20w x 60h-hole piece)
Cut 1 & work.

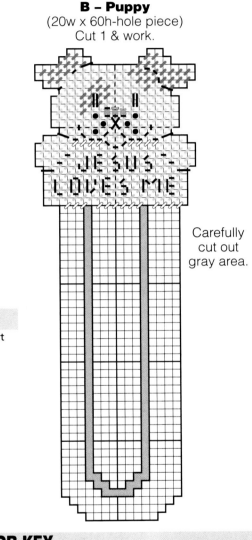

Carefully cut out gray area.

A – Kitty
(20w x 60h-hole piece)
Cut 1 & work.

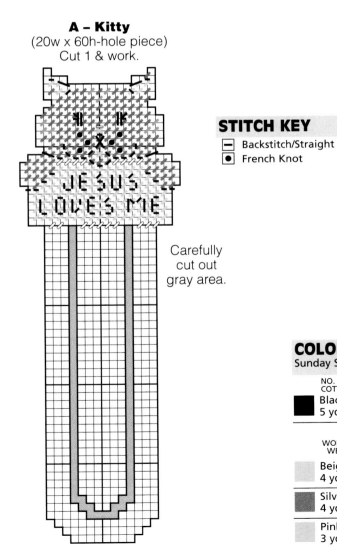

Carefully cut out gray area.

STITCH KEY
- ▬ Backstitch/Straight
- ⊙ French Knot

COLOR KEY
Sunday School Bible Bookmarks

NO. 5 PEARL COTTON	DMC®	WORSTED-WEIGHT	NEED-LOFT®
■ Black 5 yds. [4.6m]	#310	□ White 3 yds. [2.7m]	#41

	WORSTED-WEIGHT	NEED-LOFT®		
	Beige 4 yds. [3.7m]	#40	▨ Baby Blue 2 yds. [1.8m]	#36
	■ Silver 4 yds. [3.7m]	#37	■ Camel 2 yds. [1.8m]	#43
	Pink 3 yds. [2.7m]	#07	▨ Gray 1 yd. [0.9m]	#38

Church Clip

Designed by Janelle Giese

SIZE
Motif is 4¾" x 7½" [12.1cm x 19cm]

SKILL LEVEL
Average

MATERIALS
• ½ Sheet of 7-mesh QuickCount® Plastic Canvas
• One 3½"-wide [8.9cm] bag clip
• One ½" [13mm] silver liberty bell
• Craft glue of glue gun
• No. 3 Pearl Cotton (coton perlé) Art. 115 by DMC® (for amount see Color Key)
• No. 5 Pearl Cotton (coton perlé) Art. 116 by DMC® (for amount see Color Key)
• Medium #16 Metallic Braid by Kreinik (for amount see Color Key)
• Needloft® Plastic Canvas Yarn by Uniek Inc. or worsted yarn (for amounts see Color Key)

CUTTING INSTRUCTIONS
For Church Motif, cut one according to graph.

STITCHING INSTRUCTIONS
1: Using colors and stitches indicated, work piece according to graph; with matching colors as shown in photo, overcast cutout and outer edges.

2: Using colors (Hold one strand of No. 5 pearl cotton and one strand of metallic braid together as one for "Love.") and embroidery stitches indicated, embroider detail on piece as indicated on graph.

3: Tack bell inside cutout as shown. Glue bag clip to wrong side of Motif.

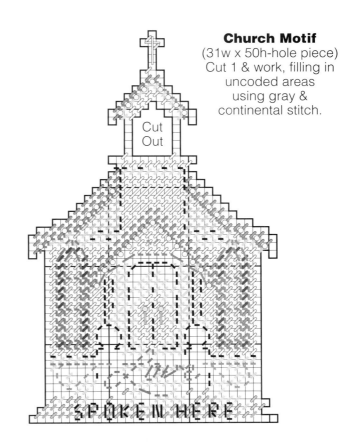

Church Motif
(31w x 50h-hole piece)
Cut 1 & work, filling in uncoded areas using gray & continental stitch.

STITCH KEY
- ▬ Backstitch/Straight
- ● French Knot

COLOR KEY
Church Clip

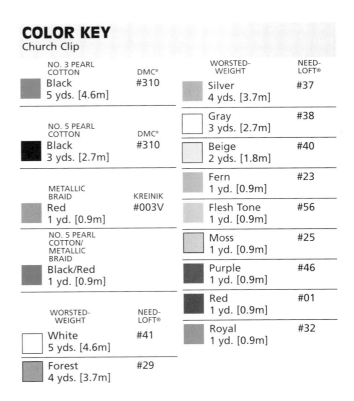

NO. 3 PEARL COTTON	DMC®
Black 5 yds. [4.6m]	#310

NO. 5 PEARL COTTON	DMC®
Black 3 yds. [2.7m]	#310

METALLIC BRAID	KREINIK
Red 1 yd. [0.9m]	#003V

NO. 5 PEARL COTTON/ METALLIC BRAID	
Black/Red 1 yd. [0.9m]	

WORSTED-WEIGHT	NEED-LOFT®
White 5 yds. [4.6m]	#41
Forest 4 yds. [3.7m]	#29

WORSTED-WEIGHT	NEED-LOFT®
Silver 4 yds. [3.7m]	#37
Gray 3 yds. [2.7m]	#38
Beige 2 yds. [1.8m]	#40
Fern 1 yd. [0.9m]	#23
Flesh Tone 1 yd. [0.9m]	#56
Moss 1 yd. [0.9m]	#25
Purple 1 yd. [0.9m]	#46
Red 1 yd. [0.9m]	#01
Royal 1 yd. [0.9m]	#32

"Jesus Loves Me" Doorknob Hanger

Designed by Cynthia Roberts

SIZE
Hanger is 4½" x 10½" [11.4cm x 26.7cm] with a 2¾" x 2¾" [7cm x 7cm] photo window

SKILL LEVEL
Easy

MATERIALS
• ½ sheet of 7-mesh plastic canvas
• Worsted-weight or plastic canvas yarn (for amounts see Color Key)

CUTTING INSTRUCTIONS
A: For Front, cut one according to graph.
B: For Backing, cut one 24w x 27h-holes (no graph).

STITCHING INSTRUCTIONS
NOTE: B is not worked.

1: Using colors and stitches indicated, work A according to graph; with light blue, overcast cutout and outer edges.

2: Center Backing over cutout on wrong side of Front and glue three edges of Backing to Front, leaving an opening at top for photo insertion.

COLOR KEY
"Jesus Loves Me"
Doorknob Hanger

WORSTED-WEIGHT

White	20 yds. [18.3m]
Lt. Blue	10 yds. [9.1m]
Lt. Green	2 yds. [1.8m]
Peach	2 yds. [1.8m]
Yellow	1 yd. [0.9m]

A – Front
(30w x 69h-hole piece)
Cut 1 & work; filling in uncoded
areas using white & continental stitch.

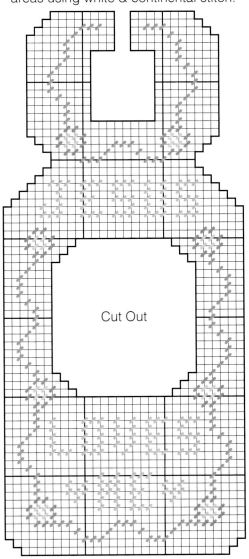

Cut Out

Rosary/Trinket Boxes

Designed by Angie Arickx

SIZE
Each Box is 3¼" x 3¼" x 1" [8.3cm x 8.3cm x 2.5cm]

SKILL LEVEL
Easy

MATERIALS FOR ONE
- ½ sheet of 7-mesh plastic canvas
- Metallic plastic canvas cord or worsted yarn (for amount see Color Key)
- Worsted-weight or plastic canvas yarn (for amounts see Color Key)

CUTTING INSTRUCTIONS
A: For Lid Top, cut one 21w x 21h-holes.
B: For Lid Sides, cut four 21w x 4h-holes.
C: For Box Sides, cut four 19w x 5h-holes.
D: For Box Bottom, cut one 19w x 19h-holes.

STITCHING INSTRUCTIONS
1: Using colors of choice and stitches indicated, work pieces according to graphs.

2: Using surface color and straight stitch, embroider detail on A as indicated on graph.

3: With background color #1, whipstitch short edges of A pieces wrong sides together and to B, forming Lid; whipstitch short edges of C pieces wrong sides together and to D, forming Box. Overcast unfinished edges.

A – Lid Top
(21w x 21h-hole piece)
Cut 1 & work.

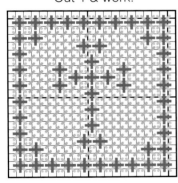

B – Lid Side
(21w x 4h-hole pieces)
Cut 4 & work.

C – Box Side
(19w x 5h-hole pieces)
Cut 4 & work.

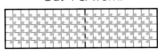

D – Box Bottom
(19w x 19h-hole piece)
Cut 1 & work.

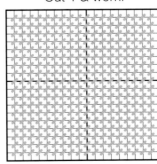

COLOR KEY
Rosary/Trinket Boxes

METALLIC CORD

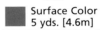

Surface Color
5 yds. [4.6m]

WORSTED-WEIGHT

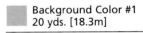

Background Color #1
20 yds. [18.3m]

Background Color #2
5 yds. [4.6m]

STITCH KEY
- Straight

Prayer Book

Designed by Nancy Barrett

SIZE
Book is 1¼" x 6⅜" x 11⅛" [3.2cm x 16.2cm x 28.3cm]

SKILL LEVEL
Average

MATERIALS
- Two sheets of 10-mesh plastic canvas
- ½ yd. [0.5m] blue ⅜" [10mm] satin ribbon
- Craft glue or glue gun
- Worsted-weight or plastic canvas yarn
  (for amounts see Color Key)

CUTTING INSTRUCTIONS
  A: For Pages, cut one 92w x 55h-holes.
  B: For Ends, cut two 55w x 10h-holes.
  C: For Top and Bottom, cut two (one for Top and one for Bottom) according to graph.
  D: For Back, cut one 111w x 64h-holes.
  E: For Butterflies, cut two according to graph.
  F: For Petals, cut sixteen according to graph.
  G: For Leaves, cut four according to graph.

STITCHING INSTRUCTIONS
 1: Using colors (Separate yarn into two plies.) and stitches indicated, work pieces according to graphs; with matching colors, overcast edges of D-G pieces.

2: Using black and straight stitch, embroider detail on E pieces as indicated on graph.

3: With white, whipstitch A-C pieces wrong sides together as indicated on graphs; with royal, whipstitch Page assembly to D as indicated.

4: For lt. blue Flowers (make 2), with yellow, tack four matching color petals together as shown in photo. For pink Flowers (make 2), with white, tack four matching color petals together as shown.

5: Arrange Flowers, Butterflies and Leaves in opposite corners of Pages as shown or as desired; glue to secure. Fold ribbon in half; glue fold to center top of Pages (see photo). Trim ends as desired.

E – Butterfly
(5w x 6h-hole pieces)
Cut 2 & work.

F – Petal
(3w x 4h-hole pieces)
Cut 16. Work 8; substituting lt. blue for pink, work 8.

G – Leaf
(5w x 6h-hole pieces)
Cut 4 & work.

COLOR KEY
Prayer Book

WORSTED-WEIGHT		WORSTED-WEIGHT	
	White 60 yds. [54.9m]		Pink 1 yd. [0.9m]
	Royal 30 yds. [27.4m]		Yellow 1 yd. [0.9m]
	Green 1 yd. [0.9m]		Black ¼ yd. [0.2m]
	Lt. Blue 1 yd. [0.9m]		

B – End
(55w x 10h-hole pieces) Cut 2 & work.

Whipstitch to A.

Whipstitch to one C.

Whipstitch to one C.

Whipstitch to D.

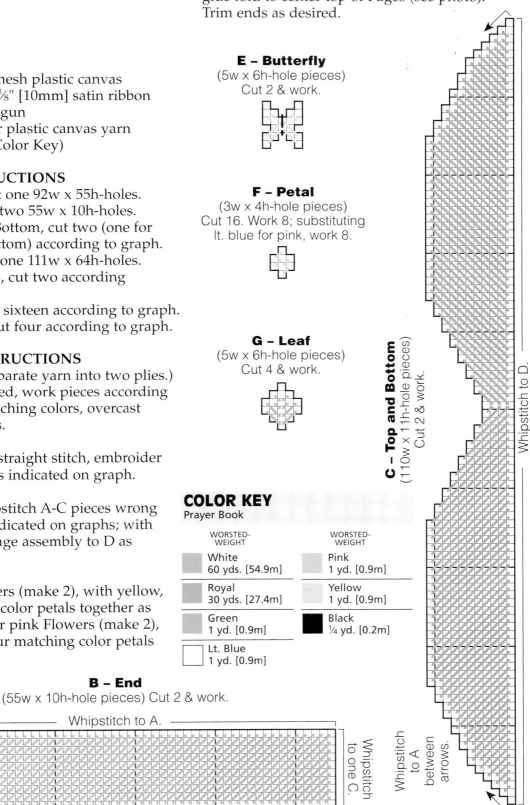

C – Top and Bottom
(110w x 11h-hole pieces)
Cut 2 & work.

Whipstitch to D.

Whipstitch to A between arrows.

D – Back

(111w x 64h-hole piece) Cut 1 & work, leaving uncoded area unworked.

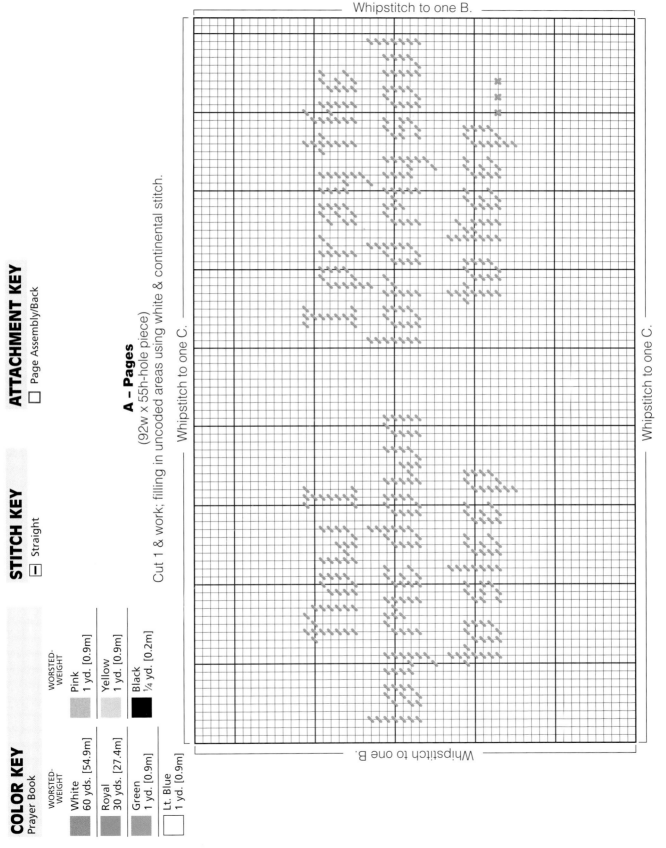

A – Pages
(92w x 55h-hole piece)
Cut 1 & work; filling in uncoded areas using white & continental stitch.

Whipstitch to one B.

Whipstitch to one C.

Whipstitch to one C.

Whipstitch to one B.

Psalm 23:1

Designed by Mary Alice Patsko

SIZE
10½" x 13½" [26.7cm x 34.3cm], not including frame

SKILL LEVEL
Average

MATERIALS FOR ONE
- One sheet of 7-mesh plastic canvas
- Worsted-weight or plastic canvas yarn (for amounts see Color Key)

CUTTING INSTRUCTIONS
For Psalm 23:1, use one sheet canvas.

STITCHING INSTRUCTIONS
1: Using colors and stitches indicated (Leave ⅜" [10mm] loops on modified turkey work stitches.), work piece according to graph.

2: Using colors and embroidery stitches indicated, embroider detail on piece as indicated on graph.

3: Frame as desired.

Psalm 23:1

(90w x 70h-hole piece)

Work, filling in uncoded areas using off white & continental stitch.

COLOR KEY
Psalm 23:1

WORSTED-WEIGHT		WORSTED-WEIGHT	
☐	Off White 3 oz. [85.1g]	▨	Green 5 yds. [4.6m]
■	Purple 10 yds. [9.1m]	▨	Lt. Green 4 yds. [3.7m]
▨	White 10 yds. [9.1m]	■	Brown 2 yds. [1.8m]
■	Gray 8 yds. [7.3m]	▨	Black ½ yd. [0.5m]

STITCH KEY
- ▬ Backstitch/Straight
- ● French Knot
- ⊗ Modified Turkey Work

Heavenly Creations 59

Perpetual Prayer Calendar

Designed by Angie Arickx

SIZE
1½" x 11½" x 5¾" tall [3.8cm x 29.2cm x 14.6cm]

SKILL LEVEL
Average

MATERIALS
•1½ sheets of 7-mesh plastic canvas
•Craft glue or glue gun
• Six-strand Embroidery Floss Art. 117 by DMC® (for amounts see Color Key)
•Needloft® Plastic Canvas Yarn by Uniek Inc. or worsted yarn (for amounts see Color Key)

CUTTING INSTRUCTIONS
A: For Calendar Front, cut one according to graph.

B: For Calendar Back, cut one according to graph.

C: For Calendar Sides, cut two 10w x 10h-holes (no graph).

D: For Calendar Bottom, cut one 40w x 10h-holes (no graph).

E: For Angel Bodies #1 and #2, cut one each according to graphs.

F: For Angel Arms, cut two according to graph.

G: For Angel Wings, cut two according to graph.

H: For Month Motifs #1, #2, #3, #4, #5 and #6, cut one each 22w x 9h-holes.

I: For Day Motifs, cut twelve 7w x 9h-holes (no graph).

STITCHING INSTRUCTIONS
NOTE: D is not worked.

1: Using colors and stitches indicated, work A, B and E-H pieces according to graphs; using bright blue and continental stitch, work C and I pieces. With matching colors and as shown in photo, overcast E-I pieces.

2: Using six strands floss and yarn (Separate into individual plies if desired.) in colors and embroidery stitches indicated, embroider detail on B, G and H pieces as indicated on graphs.

3: For each Day Motif (**Note:** *Make one 0, two 1's, two 2's and one of each 3-9.*), center and stitch one number (See Number Graph.) on each I.

4: With bright blue, whipstitch short edges of A and C pieces wrong sides together and to D as indicated. Whipstitch Sides and Bottom to B as indicated; with matching colors, overcast unfinished edges.

5: Glue corresponding Angel Arm and Angel Wing to Angel Body as shown. Glue Angels to right side of Calendar Back (see photo).

E – Angel Body #1
(12w x 21h-hole piece)
Cut 1 & work.

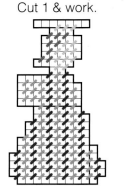

E – Angel Body #2
(12w x 21h-hole piece)
Cut 1 & work.

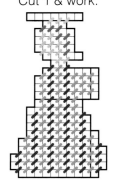

F – Angel Arm
(7w x 8h-hole pieces)
Cut 2. Work 1 &
1 reversed.

G – Angel Wing
(8w x 10h-hole pieces)
Cut 2. Work 1 & 1
reversed; filling in uncoded
areas using white &
continental stitch.

Number Graph

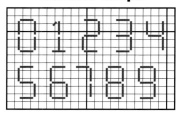

A – Calendar Front
(40w x 10h-hole piece)
Cut 1 & work.

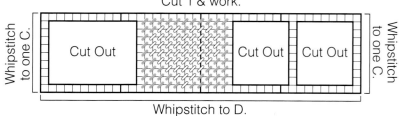

STITCH KEY
- ⊟ Backstitch/Straight
- ⊡ French Knot

B – Calendar Back
(64w x 37h-hole piece)
Cut 1 & work; filling in uncoded areas using white & continental stitch.

ATTACHMENT KEY
☐ Calendar Sides/Calendar Back

Whipstitch to D.

H – Month Motif #1
(22w x 9h-hole piece)
Cut 1 & work.

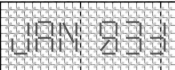

H – Month Motif #2
(22w x 9h-hole piece)
Cut 1 & work.

H – Month Motif #3
(22w x 9h-hole piece)
Cut 1 & work.

H – Month Motif #4
(22w x 9h-hole piece)
Cut 1 & work.

H – Month Motif #5
(22w x 9h-hole piece)
Cut 1 & work.

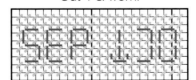

H – Month Motif #6
(22w x 9h-hole piece)
Cut 1 & work.

COLOR KEY
Perpetual Prayer Calendar

	6-STRAND FLOSS	DMC®		WORSTED-WEIGHT	NEED-LOFT®
■	Black 5 yds. [4.6m]	#310	■	Dark Royal 15 yds. [13.7m]	#48
	WORSTED-WEIGHT	NEED-LOFT®		Royal 6 yds. [5.5m]	#32
	Bright Blue 60 yds. [54.9m]	#60		Camel 1 yd. [0.9m]	#43
☐	White 25 yds. [22.9m]	#41		Flesh Tone 1 yd. [0.9m]	#56
				Yellow 1 yd. [0.9m]	#57

Inspirational Bible

Designed by Fran Rohus

SIZE
1⅜" x 8¾" x 13½" [3.5cm x 22.2cm x 34.3cm], not including Flowers

SKILL LEVEL
Challenging

MATERIALS
• Three sheets of 7-mesh plastic canvas
• ⅓ yd. [0.3m] gold ⅜" [10mm] metallic ribbon
• Craft glue or glue gun
• Metallic cord (for amount see Color Key)
• Worsted-weight or plastic canvas yarn
  (for amounts see Color Key)

CUTTING INSTRUCTIONS
   A: For Left and Right Pages, cut one each 40w x 55h-holes.
   B: For Back, cut one 89w x 57h-holes.
   C: For Tops and Bottoms, cut four (two for Tops and two for Bottoms) according to graph.
   D: For Ends, cut two 10w x 55h-holes.
   E: For Letters "W", Letter "E" and Letters "G", cut number indicated on graphs.
   F: For Flower Petals, cut four according to graph.
   G: For Flower Centers, cut four according to graph.
   H: For Leaves, cut nine according to graph.

STITCHING INSTRUCTIONS
NOTE: B is not worked.

1: Using colors and stitches indicated, work A and C-H pieces according to graphs; with cord for letters, dk. brown for Back and with matching colors, overcast B, E, G and H pieces.

2: Using black (Separate into individual plies, if desired.) and embroidery stitches indicated, embroider detail on A pieces as indicated on graphs.

3: With watermelon, overcast two F pieces; with orange and plum, overcast one remaining F in each color. For each flower, spiral one F and glue to secure according to Flower Assembly Diagram on page 66; glue one G to center of each flower.

4: With eggshell, whipstitch A-D pieces together as indicated and according to Book Assembly Diagram on page 66. Glue one end of ribbon to center top; trim other end of ribbon as desired or as shown in photo. Glue letters, Flowers and Leaves to pages as shown.

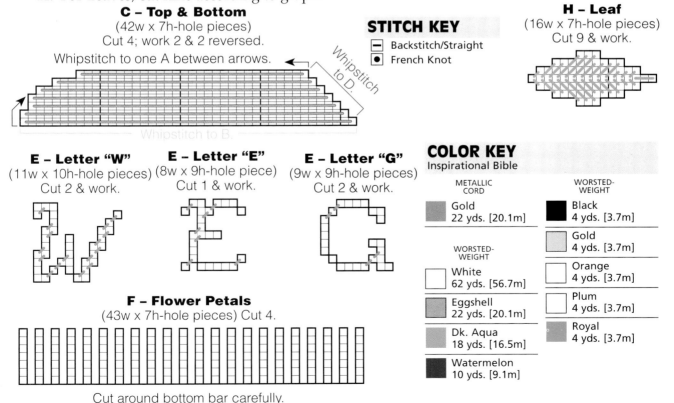

C – Top & Bottom
(42w x 7h-hole pieces)
Cut 4; work 2 & 2 reversed.
Whipstitch to one A between arrows.
Whipstitch to D.
Whipstitch to B.

STITCH KEY
⊟ Backstitch/Straight
⊡ French Knot

H – Leaf
(16w x 7h-hole pieces)
Cut 9 & work.

E – Letter "W"
(11w x 10h-hole pieces)
Cut 2 & work.

E – Letter "E"
(8w x 9h-hole piece)
Cut 1 & work.

E – Letter "G"
(9w x 9h-hole pieces)
Cut 2 & work.

F – Flower Petals
(43w x 7h-hole pieces) Cut 4.
Cut around bottom bar carefully.

COLOR KEY
Inspirational Bible

METALLIC CORD		WORSTED-WEIGHT	
Gold 22 yds. [20.1m]		Black 4 yds. [3.7m]	
WORSTED-WEIGHT		Gold 4 yds. [3.7m]	
White 62 yds. [56.7m]		Orange 4 yds. [3.7m]	
Eggshell 22 yds. [20.1m]		Plum 4 yds. [3.7m]	
Dk. Aqua 18 yds. [16.5m]		Royal 4 yds. [3.7m]	
Watermelon 10 yds. [9.1m]			

A – Right Page
(40w x 55h-hole pieces)
Cut 1 & work, filling in uncoded areas
using white & continental stitch.

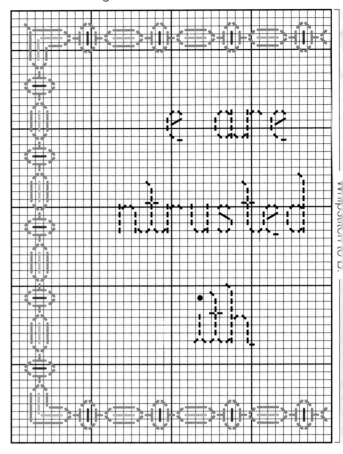

A – Left Page
(40w x 55h-hole pieces)
Cut 1 & work, filling in uncoded areas
using white & continental stitch.

Whipstitch to B.

Book Assembly Diagram
(Pieces are shown in different colors for contrast.)

Step 1:
Whipstitch
center
edges of A
pieces to
center of
B.

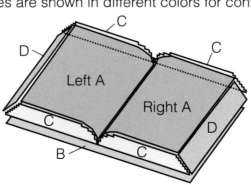

Left A

Right A

C

D

C

C

B

C

D

Step 2:
Whipstitch
C and D
pieces to
B;
Whipstitch
C, D and A
pieces
together.

Flower Assembly Diagram

Step 1:
Hold F with individual
petals at a slight angle.

F

Bottom Bar

Step 2:
Beginning at one end, spiral
bottom bar of F around the
center point, gluing to secure
as you work.

(Actual
spiral will
be more
tightly
coiled.)

COLOR KEY
Inspirational Bible

METALLIC CORD

Gold
22 yds. [20.1m]

WORSTED-WEIGHT

White
62 yds. [56.7m]

Eggshell
22 yds. [20.1m]

Dk. Aqua
18 yds. [16.5m]

Watermelon
10 yds. [9.1m]

WORSTED-WEIGHT

Black
4 yds. [3.7m]

Gold
4 yds. [3.7m]

Orange
4 yds. [3.7m]

Plum
4 yds. [3.7m]

Royal
4 yds. [3.7m]

STITCH KEY
– Backstitch/Straight
● French Knot

G – Flower Center
(4w x 4h-hole pieces)
Cut 4 & work.

ATTACHMENT KEY
☐ Left Page/Back
☐ Right Page/Back
☐ Page End
☐ Page Top & Bottom

D – End
(10w x 55h-hole pieces)
Cut 2 & work.

Whipstitch to C

Whipstitch to C

B – Back
(89w x 57h-hole piece)
Cut 1 & leave unworked.

Top edge of Book.

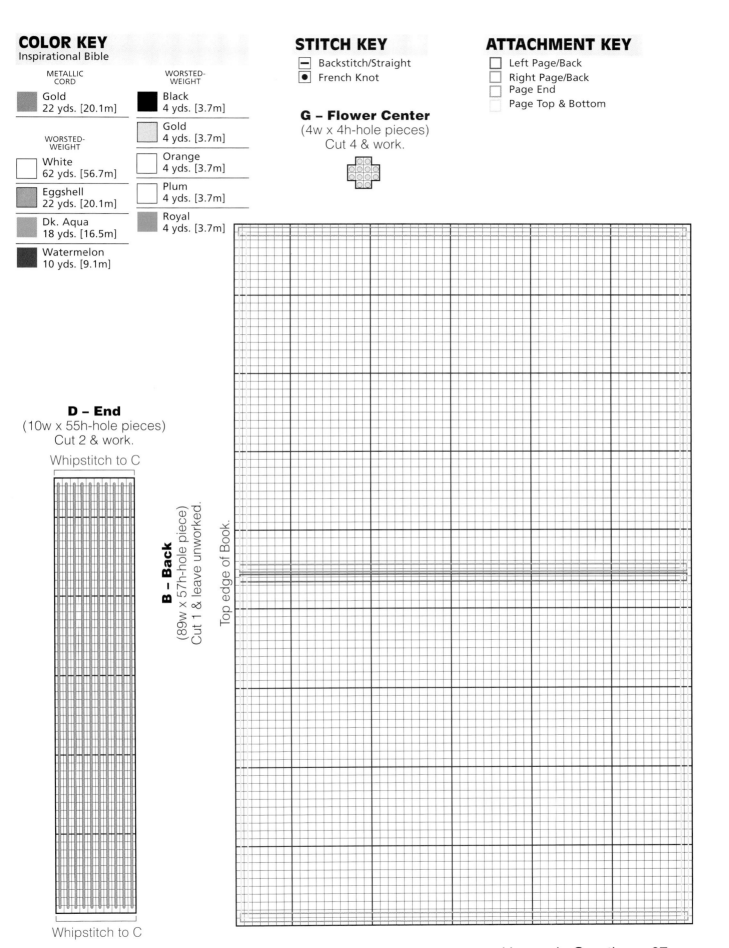

Band of *Angels*

Our friends are like angels
who brighten our days
In all kinds of wonderful,
magical ways.
Their thoughtfulness comes
as a gift from above,
And we feel we're surrounded
by warm, caring love.
Friends are like angels
without any wings,
Blessing our lives with
the most precious things.

Author Unknown

Chapter Three

Angel Fridgies
Designed by Janelle Giese

SIZES
Each Magnet is 4" x 4⅜" [10.2cm x 11.1cm]

SKILL LEVEL
Average

MATERIALS FOR ALL
• ½ Sheet of 7-mesh QuickCount® Plastic
  Canvas by Uniek Inc.
• 1 yd. [0.9m] white ⅛" [3mm] satin ribbon
• Three ¾" [19mm] button magnets
• Craft glue or glue gun
• Six-strand Embroidery Floss Art. 117 by
  DMC® (for amount see Color Key)
• No. 8 Pearl Cotton (coton perlé) Art. 118
  by DMC® (for amount see Color Key)
• Heavy #32 Metallic Braid by Kreinik
  (for amount see Color Key)
• Needloft® Plastic Canvas Yarn by Uniek Inc.
  or worsted yarn (for amounts see Color Key)

CUTTING INSTRUCTIONS
A: For Faith, cut one according to graph.
B: For Hope, cut one according to graph.
C: For Love, cut one according to graph.
D: For Cross, cut one according to graph.
E: For Candle, cut one according to graph.
F: For Heart, cut one according to graph.

STITCHING INSTRUCTIONS
1: Using colors and stitches indicated, work
pieces according to graphs; with vatican
for Candle, lavender for Heart and with
matching colors as shown in photo, overcast
edges of pieces.

2: Using colors and embroidery stitches
indicated, embroider detail on A-C and E
pieces as indicated on graphs.

3: Cut ribbon into four equal lengths;
insert one end of one ribbon from front to
back through ◆ hole on A, leaving a 1½"
[3.8cm] tail at back of piece; thread remaining
end of ribbon from front to back through
remaining ◆ hole leaving a 1½" [3.8cm] tail at
back of piece. Repeat with two ribbon lengths
and B and C pieces.

4: Glue Cross to right side of Faith, Candle to
right side of Hope and Heart to right side of
Love as shown in photo. Tie remaining ribbon
length into a bow; glue to right side of Candle
as shown. Glue one magnet to wrong side of
each Angel.

A – Faith
(26w x 29h-hole piece)
Cut 1 & work.

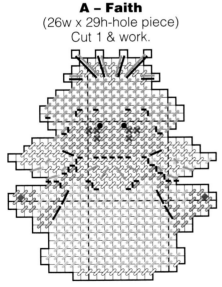

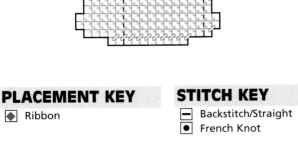

PLACEMENT KEY
◆ Ribbon

STITCH KEY
– Backstitch/Straight
● French Knot

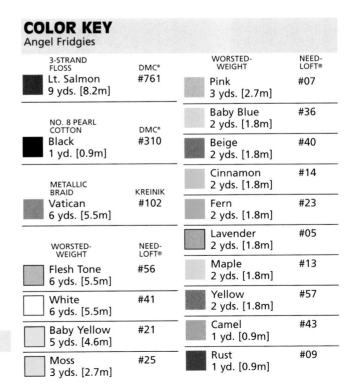

COLOR KEY
Angel Fridgies

	3-STRAND FLOSS	DMC®		WORSTED-WEIGHT	NEED-LOFT®
■	Lt. Salmon 9 yds. [8.2m]	#761	▨	Pink 3 yds. [2.7m]	#07

	NO. 8 PEARL COTTON	DMC®		Baby Blue 2 yds. [1.8m]	#36
■	Black 1 yd. [0.9m]	#310	▨	Beige 2 yds. [1.8m]	#40

	METALLIC BRAID	KREINIK		Cinnamon 2 yds. [1.8m]	#14
▨	Vatican 6 yds. [5.5m]	#102	▨	Fern 2 yds. [1.8m]	#23

	WORSTED-WEIGHT	NEED-LOFT®		Lavender 2 yds. [1.8m]	#05
▨	Flesh Tone 6 yds. [5.5m]	#56	▨	Maple 2 yds. [1.8m]	#13
□	White 6 yds. [5.5m]	#41	▨	Yellow 2 yds. [1.8m]	#57
□	Baby Yellow 5 yds. [4.6m]	#21	▨	Camel 1 yd. [0.9m]	#43
▨	Moss 3 yds. [2.7m]	#25	▨	Rust 1 yd. [0.9m]	#09

B – Hope
(26w x 29h-hole piece)
Cut 1 & work.

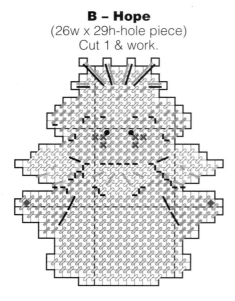

COLOR KEY
Angel Fridgies

3-STRAND FLOSS	DMC®		WORSTED-WEIGHT	NEED-LOFT®
Lt. Salmon 9 yds. [8.2m]	#761		Pink 3 yds. [2.7m]	#07
NO. 8 PEARL COTTON	DMC®		Baby Blue 2 yds. [1.8m]	#36
Black 1 yd. [0.9m]	#310		Beige 2 yds. [1.8m]	#40
METALLIC BRAID	KREINIK		Cinnamon 2 yds. [1.8m]	#14
Vatican 6 yds. [5.5m]	#102		Fern 2 yds. [1.8m]	#23
			Lavender 2 yds. [1.8m]	#05
WORSTED-WEIGHT	NEED-LOFT®		Maple 2 yds. [1.8m]	#13
Flesh tone 6 yds. [5.5m]	#56		Yellow 2 yds. [1.8m]	#57
White 6 yds. [5.5m]	#41		Camel 1 yd. [0.9m]	#43
Baby Yellow 5 yds. [4.6m]	#21		Rust 1 yd. [0.9m]	#09
Moss 3 yds. [2.7m]	#25			

C – Love
(26w x 29h-hole piece)
Cut 1 & work.

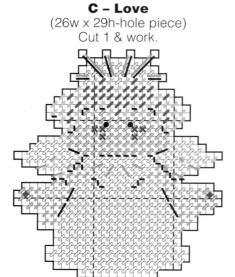

PLACEMENT KEY
◆ Ribbon

STITCH KEY
— Backstitch/Straight
● French Knot

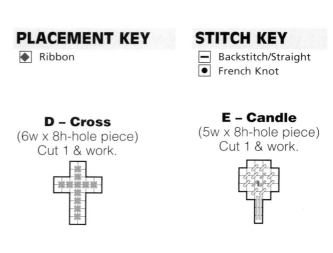

D – Cross
(6w x 8h-hole piece)
Cut 1 & work.

E – Candle
(5w x 8h-hole piece)
Cut 1 & work.

F – Heart
(7w x 6h-hole piece)
Cut 1 & work.

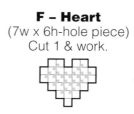

Angel Ornament

Designed by Kathy Wirth

SIZE
5" x 6" [12.7cm x 15.2cm]

SKILL LEVEL
Average

MATERIALS
- ½ sheet of 10-mesh plastic canvas
- ¼ yd. [0.2m] of gold ⅜" [10mm] ribbon
- ⅔ yd. [0.6m] of gold metallic wired foil Christmas trim with stars
- Craft glue or glue gun
- Six-strand embroidery floss (for amount see Color Key)
- 1/16" [2mm] Metallic Ribbon by Kreinik (for amounts see Color Key)
- No. 3 Pearl Cotton (coton perlé) by Anchor® (for amounts see Color Key)

CUTTING INSTRUCTIONS
   A: For Head, cut one according to graph.
   B: For Dress, cut one according to graph.
   C: For Arm, cut two according to graph.
   D: For Left Foot, cut one according to graph.
   E: For Right Foot, cut one according to graph.
   F: For Wings, cut one according to graph.

STITCHING INSTRUCTIONS
1: Using colors and stitches indicated, work pieces according to graphs; with gold for Wings and with matching colors, overcast edges of B-F pieces.

NOTE: Cut eleven 2" [5.1cm] lengths of salmon dk.

2: Using floss and French knot, embroider eyes on A as indicated on graph. For hair, attach one 2" [5.1cm] strand with a lark's head knot (see illustration) to each hole on A as indicated; pull ends even and fray to fluff. With matching colors, overcast edges of A.

3: Glue one Arm and Head to right side of B over unworked area; glue remaining Arm, Feet and Wings to wrong side of B as shown in photo.

NOTES: Cut one 4" [10.2cm] length of gold trim; cut off stars. Tie ribbon into a bow.

4: Glue 4" length of trim around Head for halo; twist and bend remaining length as shown or as desired and glue to Angel's hands; glue bow to front of Angel as shown. Hang as desired.

A – Head
(13w x 13h-hole piece)
Cut 1 & work.

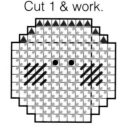

E – Right Foot
(7w x 11h-hole piece)
Cut 1 & work.

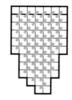

D – Left Foot
(11w x 5h-hole piece)
Cut 1 & work.

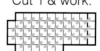

B – Dress
(35w x 39h-hole piece)
Cut 1 & work, leaving
uncoded area
unworked.

C – Arm
(13w x 21h-hole pieces)
Cut 2 & work.

F – Wings
(48w x 14h-hole piece)
Cut 1 & work.

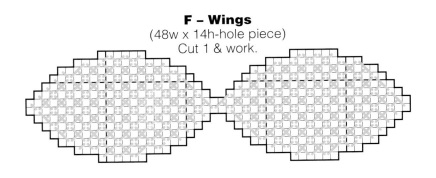

Lark's Head Knot
Stitch Illustration

STITCH KEY
- ● French Knot
- ▲ Lark's Head Knot

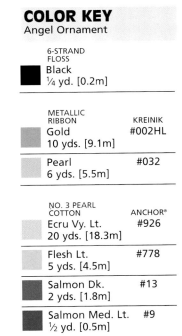

COLOR KEY
Angel Ornament

	6-STRAND FLOSS	
■	Black ¼ yd. [0.2m]	

	METALLIC RIBBON	KREINIK
	Gold 10 yds. [9.1m]	#002HL
	Pearl 6 yds. [5.5m]	#032

	NO. 3 PEARL COTTON	ANCHOR®
	Ecru Vy. Lt. 20 yds. [18.3m]	#926
	Flesh Lt. 5 yds. [4.5m]	#778
	Salmon Dk. 2 yds. [1.8m]	#13
	Salmon Med. Lt. ½ yd. [0.5m]	#9

Joy Angel

Designed by Terri Ricioli

SIZE
4" x 6¾" [10.2cm x 17.1cm]

SKILL LEVEL
Average

MATERIALS
- ½ sheet of ivory 7-mesh plastic canvas
- Craft glue or glue gun
- Six-strand embroidery floss (for amounts see Color Key)
- Needloft® Plastic Canvas Yarn by Uniek Inc. or worsted yarn (for amounts see Color Key)

CUTTING INSTRUCTIONS
A: For Body Front and Back, cut one each according to graphs.

B: For Arm Pieces, cut four according to graph.

C: For Leg Pieces, cut four according to graph.

D: For Wings, cut one according to graph.

E: For Banner Front and Back, cut one each according to graphs.

STITCHING INSTRUCTIONS
1: Using colors and stitches indicated, work pieces according to graphs. Using colors and embroidery stitches indicated, embroider detail on Front A as indicated on graph.

2: For Body, with matching colors as shown in photo, whipstitch A pieces wrong sides together as indicated on graphs; with gold, overcast unfinished edges.

3: For Arms (make 2), with matching colors, whipstitch two B pieces wrong sides together; for Legs (make 2), with flesh tone, whipstitch two corresponding pieces wrong sides together. For Banner, with eggshell, whipstitch E pieces wrong sides together.

4: Glue Legs inside opening of Body (see photo); glue Arms, Wings and Banner to Body as shown. Hang or display as desired.

A – Body Front
(28w x 18h-hole piece)
Cut 1 & work.

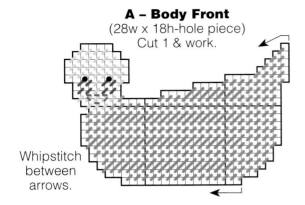

Whipstitch between arrows.

A – Body Back
(28w x 18h-hole piece)
Cut 1 & work.

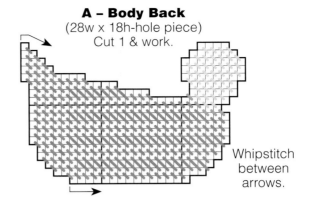

Whipstitch between arrows.

C – Leg Piece
(9w x 4h-hole pieces)
Cut 4; work 2 & 2 reversed.

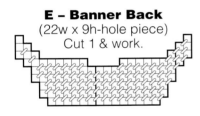

B – Arm Piece
(14w x 4h-hole pieces)
Cut 4 & work.

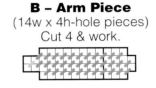

E – Banner Back
(22w x 9h-hole piece)
Cut 1 & work.

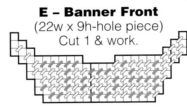

E – Banner Front
(22w x 9h-hole piece)
Cut 1 & work.

STITCH KEY

- Backstitch/Straight
- • French Knot

D – Wings
(27w x 10h-hole pieces)
Cut 1 & work, leaving uncoded areas unworked.

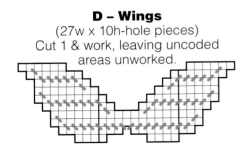

COLOR KEY
Joy Angel

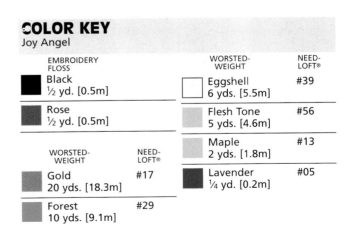

EMBROIDERY FLOSS			WORSTED-WEIGHT	NEED-LOFT®
■	Black ½ yd. [0.5m]		□ Eggshell 6 yds. [5.5m]	#39
■	Rose ½ yd. [0.5m]		Flesh Tone 5 yds. [4.6m]	#56
WORSTED-WEIGHT		NEED-LOFT®	Maple 2 yds. [1.8m]	#13
	Gold 20 yds. [18.3m]	#17	Lavender ¼ yd. [0.2m]	#05
	Forest 10 yds. [9.1m]	#29		

Angel Trio
Designed by Kathleen Hurley

SIZE
Each Angel is 5½" x 6¾" [14cm x 17.1cm]

SKILL LEVEL
Average

MATERIALS
- One sheet of 7-mesh plastic canvas
- Metallic cord (for amounts see Color Key)
- Worsted-weight or plastic canvas yarn
  (for amounts see Color Key)

CUTTING INSTRUCTIONS
    A: For Joy Angel, cut one according to graph.
    B: For Love Angel, cut one according to graph.
    C: For Noel Angel, cut one according to graph.

STITCHING INSTRUCTIONS
1: Using colors and stitches indicated, work pieces according to graphs; with matching colors as shown in photo, overcast cutouts and outer edges of pieces.

2: Using colors (Separate into individual plies if desired.) and embroidery stitches indicated, embroider detail on pieces as indicated on graphs.

3: Hang or display as desired.

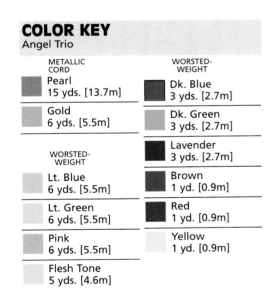

COLOR KEY
Angel Trio

METALLIC CORD		WORSTED-WEIGHT	
Pearl 15 yds. [13.7m]		Dk. Blue 3 yds. [2.7m]	
Gold 6 yds. [5.5m]		Dk. Green 3 yds. [2.7m]	
WORSTED-WEIGHT		Lavender 3 yds. [2.7m]	
Lt. Blue 6 yds. [5.5m]		Brown 1 yd. [0.9m]	
Lt. Green 6 yds. [5.5m]		Red 1 yd. [0.9m]	
Pink 6 yds. [5.5m]		Yellow 1 yd. [0.9m]	
Flesh Tone 5 yds. [4.6m]			

STITCH KEY
- ⊟ Backstitch/Straight
- ⊙ French Knot
- ⊘ Lazy Daisy

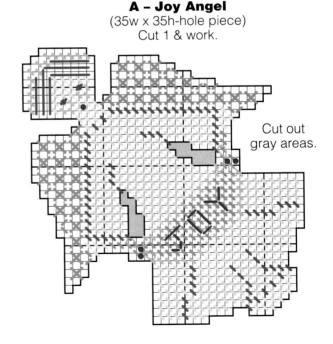

A – Joy Angel
(35w x 35h-hole piece)
Cut 1 & work.

Cut out gray areas.

B – Love Angel
(35w x 35h-hole piece)
Cut 1 & work.

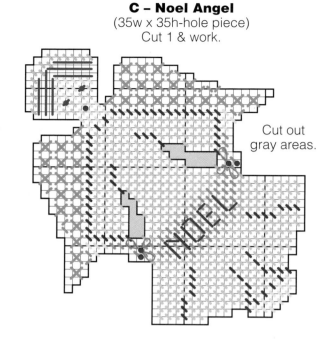

Cut out
gray areas.

C – Noel Angel
(35w x 35h-hole piece)
Cut 1 & work.

Cut out
gray areas.

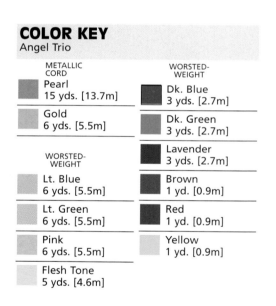

STITCH KEY
- – Backstitch/Straight
- • French Knot
- ◐ Lazy Daisy

COLOR KEY
Angel Trio

METALLIC CORD		WORSTED-WEIGHT	
Pearl	15 yds. [13.7m]	Dk. Blue	3 yds. [2.7m]
Gold	6 yds. [5.5m]	Dk. Green	3 yds. [2.7m]
WORSTED-WEIGHT		Lavender	3 yds. [2.7m]
Lt. Blue	6 yds. [5.5m]	Brown	1 yd. [0.9m]
Lt. Green	6 yds. [5.5m]	Red	1 yd. [0.9m]
Pink	6 yds. [5.5m]	Yellow	1 yd. [0.9m]
Flesh Tone	5 yds. [4.6m]		

Angel Box

Designed by Kathleen Hurley

SIZE
2⅝" x 9⅜" x 12⅜" [6.7cm x 23.8cm x 31.5cm]

SKILL LEVEL
Average

MATERIALS
• Four sheets of 7-mesh plastic canvas
• Six-strand embroidery floss (for amounts see Color Key)
• Metallic cord (for amount see Color Key)
• Worsted-weight or plastic canvas yarn (for amounts see Color Key)

CUTTING INSTRUCTIONS
A: For Lid Top, cut one 82w x 62h-holes.
B: For Lid Sides, cut two 82w x 17h-holes (no graph).
C: For Lid Ends, cut two 62w x 17h-holes (no graph).
D: For Box Sides, cut two 80w x 16h-holes (no graph).
E: For Box Ends, cut two 60w x 16h-holes (no graph).
F: For Box Bottom, cut one 80w x 60h-holes (no graph).

G: For Divider Piece #1, #2 and #3, cut one 38w x 15h-holes for Piece #1, one 41w x 15h-holes for Piece #2 and one 79w x 15h-holes for Piece #3 (no graphs).

STITCHING INSTRUCTIONS
NOTE: D-G pieces are not worked.

1: Using colors and stitches indicated, work A according to graph and B and C pieces according to Lid Side Stitch Pattern Guide.

2: Using three strands floss in colors and embroidery stitches indicated, embroider detail on A as indicated on graph.

3: With blue, whipstitch B and C pieces wrong sides together and to A, forming Lid; overcast edges.

4: With white, whipstitch D-G pieces together according to Box Assembly Diagram.

Box Assembly Diagram
(Pieces are shown in different colors for contrast.)

Step 1:
Whipstitch F & G pieces together.

Step 2:
Whipstitch D & E pieces together and to F & G pieces.

A – Lid Top
(82w x 62h-hole piece)
Cut 1 & work, filling in uncoded areas using white & continental stitch.

Lid Side Stitch Pattern Guide

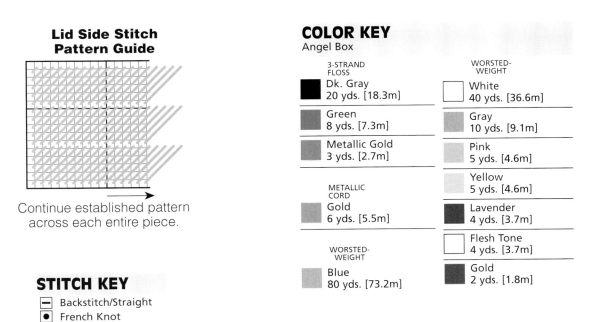

Continue established pattern across each entire piece.

STITCH KEY
- Backstitch/Straight
- French Knot

COLOR KEY
Angel Box

3-STRAND FLOSS

■	Dk. Gray	20 yds. [18.3m]
■	Green	8 yds. [7.3m]
■	Metallic Gold	3 yds. [2.7m]

METALLIC CORD

■	Gold	6 yds. [5.5m]

WORSTED-WEIGHT

■	Blue	80 yds. [73.2m]

WORSTED-WEIGHT

□	White	40 yds. [36.6m]
■	Gray	10 yds. [9.1m]
■	Pink	5 yds. [4.6m]
■	Yellow	5 yds. [4.6m]
■	Lavender	4 yds. [3.7m]
□	Flesh Tone	4 yds. [3.7m]
■	Gold	2 yds. [1.8m]

Patriotic Angel

Designed by Mary Layfield

SIZE
4½" x 10½" x 10½" tall [11.4cm x 26.7cm x 26.7cm]

SKILL LEVEL
Challenging

MATERIALS
- Five Sheets of 10-mesh Plastic Canvas by Darice®
- One Holiday Time Porcelain Head with Hands #016217 by Mengelsen's
- One 12" [30.5cm] clear plastic cone
- Two white 3mm chenille stems
- ¼ yd. [0.2m] each red and navy 44/45" [111.8/114.3cm] lace fabric with decorative selvage edge
- Thirteen ⅝" [16mm] star appliqués
- 2 yds. [1.8m] red 1½" [3.8cm] satin ribbon with wire edge
- ⅔ yd. [0.6m] gold 1" [2.5cm] metallic ribbon
- Two 6" [15.2cm] lengths of gold ½" [13mm] metallic ribbon
- Sewing needle and navy thread
- Craft glue or glue gun
- Medium #16 Metallic Braid by Kreinik (for amount see Color Key)
- Six-strand Embroidery Floss Art. 117 by DMC® (for amounts see Color Key)

CUTTING INSTRUCTIONS
A: For Bodice, cut one according to graph.
B: For Skirt Front, cut one according to graph.
C: For Skirt Back Pieces #1 and #2, cut one each according to graphs.
D: For Wings Front and Backing, cut two (one for Front and one for Backing) according to graph.

STITCHING INSTRUCTIONS
NOTE: Backing D is not worked.

1: Using colors and stitches indicated, work pieces according to graphs; with gold, overcast bottom edges of B and C pieces.

2: For Bodice, with white, whipstitch indicated edges of A wrong sides together; with gold, overcast armholes and neck areas. For Skirt, with white, whipstitch B and C pieces wrong sides together as indicated on graphs; omitting attachment area, overcast top edge. Matching center of Bodice to center of Skirt Front, whipstitch pieces right sides together as indicated; with red, overcast remaining unfinished edges.

NOTES: Cut 2" [5.1cm] off bottom edge of cone. Twist chenille stems together as shown in photo on page 87, making sure opening fits over cone 1½" [3.8cm] from top and glue in place; cut 1" [2.5cm] off end of each chenille stem and glue one arm on each chenille stem.

3: Place dress on cone, carefully pulling arms through armholes of Bodice. Place head on top of cone; glue to secure. Glue neck edge of Bodice to head. Overlap B pieces to fit snugly on cone and glue to cone to secure. Glue back of Bodice to cone.

NOTE: From each color lace fabric, cut two 6" x 9" [15.2cm x 22.9cm] pieces for sleeves and one 9" x 32/33" [22.9cm x 81.3cm/83.8cm] piece for overskirt according to Sleeve and Overskirt Cutting Illustration on page 89.

4: For sleeves (make 2), holding one navy and one red sleeve piece together as one so that navy piece is on top, sew short edges of fabric together with a ½" [13mm] seam. Gather long cut edge until it measures about 1" [2.5cm] across; tack to secure. Place gathered edge inside armhole of Bodice around arms and glue to secure. Gather 1" [2.5cm] along scalloped edge to fit tightly on wrist; tack to secure.

5: For overskirt, holding both red and navy overskirt pieces together as one, fold 9" x 32/33" pieces as indicated on Cutting Illustration making sure the navy piece is on top. Working through all thicknesses as one, gather cut edges to fit around Skirt, beginning at one dart on front of Bodice around back to remaining dart as shown in photo; glue in place. Fold gold ½" ribbon under ½" [13mm] at each end and glue ribbon to top edge of overskirt to cover all seams and gathers.

6: Tie a knot in center of gold 1" ribbon; glue knot to center back of Skirt, letting ends hang down at each side of Angel. Tie a knot in center of red ribbon; glue knot to center back of Skirt over gold ribbon knot. Pull one end to each side of Angel; make three large loops on each side of overskirt as shown and glue loops to secure.

7: For Wings, with indicated and matching colors, whipstitch Backing D to wrong side of Front D; center and glue right side of Wings to back of Angel (see photo). Glue one star appliqué over each group of navy blue stitches.

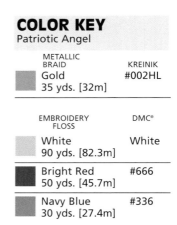

COLOR KEY
Patriotic Angel

	METALLIC BRAID	KREINIK
	Gold 35 yds. [32m]	#002HL

	EMBROIDERY FLOSS	DMC®
	White 90 yds. [82.3m]	White
	Bright Red 50 yds. [45.7m]	#666
	Navy Blue 30 yds. [27.4m]	#336

C – Skirt Back Piece #1
(51w x 72h-hole piece)
Cut 1 & work.

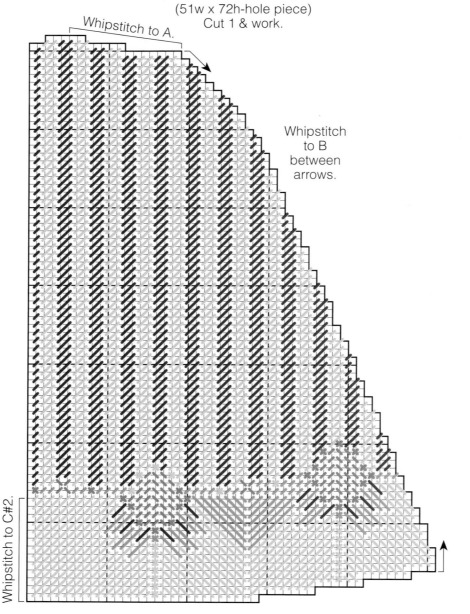

Whipstitch to A.

Whipstitch to B between arrows.

Whipstitch to C#2.

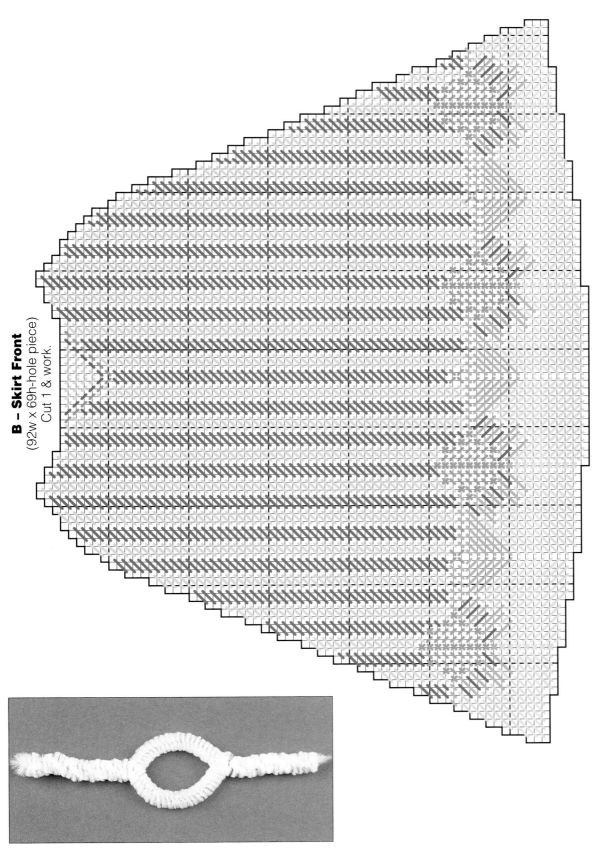

B – Skirt Front
(92w x 69h-hole piece)
Cut 1 & work.

Two Chenille Stems Twisted Together

C – Skirt Back Piece #2
(51w x 72h-hole piece)
Cut 1 & work.

Whipstitch to A.

Whipstitch
to B
between
arrows.

Whipstitch to C #1.

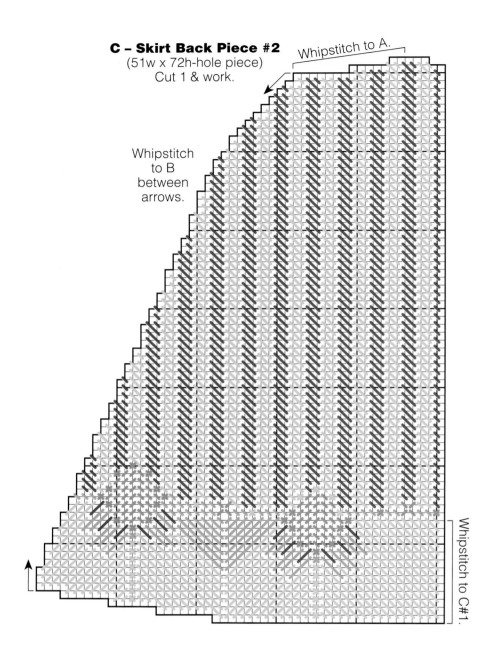

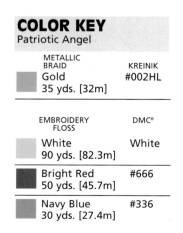

COLOR KEY
Patriotic Angel

	METALLIC BRAID	KREINIK
	Gold 35 yds. [32m]	#002HL

	EMBROIDERY FLOSS	DMC®
	White 90 yds. [82.3m]	White
	Bright Red 50 yds. [45.7m]	#666
	Navy Blue 30 yds. [27.4m]	#336

A – Bodice
(43w x 49h-hole piece) Cut 1 & work.

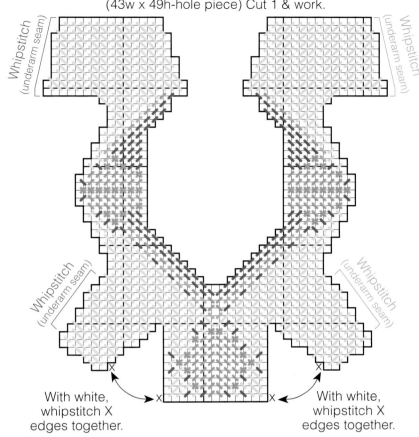

Whipstitch (underarm seam)

Whipstitch (underarm seam)

Whipstitch (underarm seam)

Whipstitch (underarm seam)

With white, whipstitch X edges together.

With white, whipstitch X edges together.

Overskirt and Sleeve
Cutting Illustration
(Pieces are shown in different colors for contrast.)

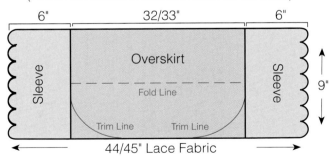

6"

32/33"

6"

Sleeve

Overskirt

Sleeve

Fold Line

Trim Line

Trim Line

9"

44/45" Lace Fabric

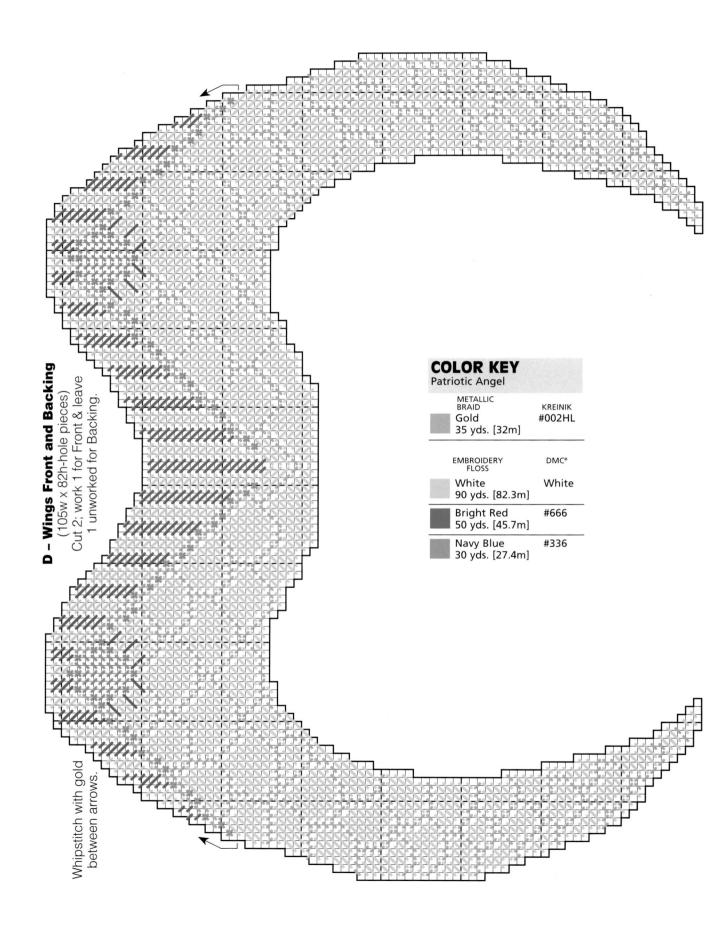

D – Wings Front and Backing
(105w x 82h-hole pieces)
Cut 2; work 1 for Front & leave
1 unworked for Backing.

Whipstitch with gold
between arrows.

COLOR KEY
Patriotic Angel

	METALLIC BRAID	KREINIK
	Gold 35 yds. [32m]	#002HL

	EMBROIDERY FLOSS	DMC®
	White 90 yds. [82.3m]	White
	Bright Red 50 yds. [45.7m]	#666
	Navy Blue 30 yds. [27.4m]	#336

Angel With Stars

Designed by Kristine Loffredo

SIZE
11¼" x 11½" [28.6cm x 29.2cm]

SKILL LEVEL
Average

MATERIALS
• One Sheet of 7-mesh QuickCount® Plastic Canvas by Uniek Inc.
• Two Plastic Canvas QuickShape™ 6" [15.2cm] Heart Shapes by Uniek Inc.
• Three Plastic Canvas QuickShape™ 5" [12.7cm] Star Shapes by Uniek Inc.
• Craft glue or glue gun
• Needloft® Plastic Canvas Yarn by Uniek Inc. or worsted yarn (for amounts see Color Key)

CUTTING INSTRUCTIONS
A: For Angel, cut one according to graph.

B: For Stars, cut three from star shapes according to graph.

C: For Wings, cut two from heart shapes according to graph.

STITCHING INSTRUCTIONS
1: Using colors and stitches indicated, work pieces according to graphs; with matching colors as shown in photo, overcast cutout on A and edges of A-C pieces.

2: Using colors (Separate into individual plies if desired.) and embroidery stitches indicated, embroider detail on A as indicated on graph.

3: Glue Stars to right side of Angel and Wings to wrong side of Angel as shown. Display as desired.

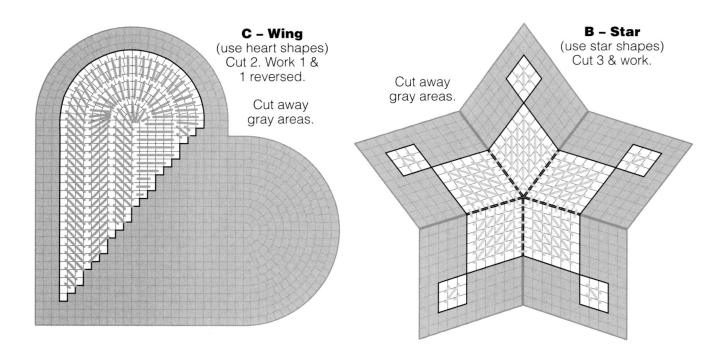

C – Wing
(use heart shapes)
Cut 2. Work 1 & 1 reversed.

Cut away gray areas.

B – Star
(use star shapes)
Cut 3 & work.

Cut away gray areas.

A – Angel
(70w x 71h-hole piece)
Cut 1 & work.

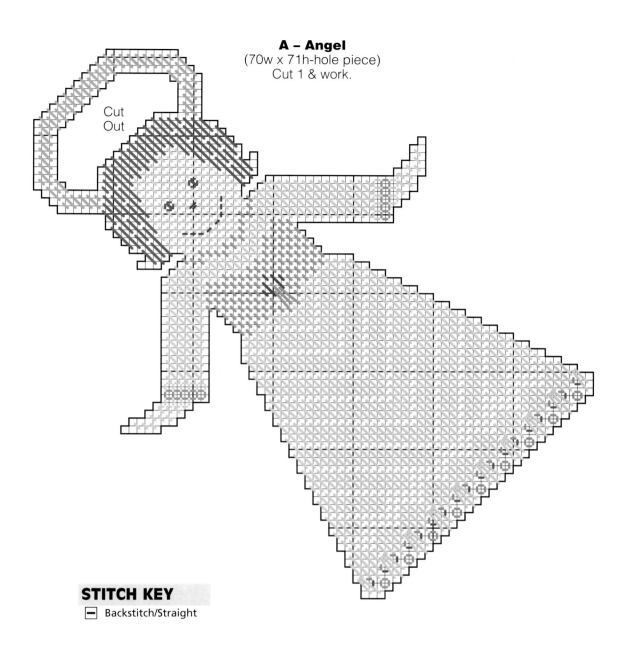

Cut
Out

STITCH KEY
– Backstitch/Straight

COLOR KEY
Angel With Stars

METALLIC BRAID	NEED-LOFT®	WORSTED-WEIGHT	NEED-LOFT®
Gold 5 yds. [4.6m]	#01	Brown 3 yds. [2.7m]	#15
Green 4 yds. [3.7m]	#04	Flesh Tone 2 yds. [1.8m]	#56
WORSTED-WEIGHT	**NEED-LOFT®**	Lavender ½ yd. [0.5m]	#05
White 25 yds. [22.9m]	#41	Burgundy ¼ yd. [0.2m]	#03
Yellow 15 yds. [13.7m]	#57	Dark Royal ¼ yd. [0.2m]	#48
Bright Blue 10 yds. [9.1m]	#60		

Angel of Mercy

Designed by Mary Layfield

SIZE
4½" x 10½" x 10½" tall [11.4cm x 26.7cm x 26.7cm]

SKILL LEVEL
Challenging

MATERIALS
- Five Sheets of 10-mesh Plastic Canvas by Darice®
- One Holiday Time Porcelain Head with Hands #016217 by Mengelsen's
- One 12" [30.5cm] clear plastic cone
- Two white 3mm chenille stems
- 20" [50.8cm] length each of white 2" [5.1cm] double-layered gathered lace and white ½" [13mm] single layer gathered lace
- ¼ yd. [0.2m] white 5"-wide [12.7cm] gathered lace
- 1 yd. [0.9m] gold ⅜" [10mm] ribbon with wired edge
- 6" [15.2cm] length of gold ⅛" [3mm] metallic ribbon
- 1½ yds. [1.4m] burgundy 1½" [3.8cm] ribbon with wire edge
- Twenty-four assorted-color small silk flowers
- Craft glue or glue gun
- No. 3 Pearl Cotton (coton perlé) Art. 115 by DMC® (for amounts see Color Key)

CUTTING INSTRUCTIONS
A: For Bodice, cut one according to graph.
B: For Skirt Front, cut one according to graph.
C: For Skirt Back Pieces, cut two according to graph.
D: For Overskirt Pieces #1, #2 and #3, cut one each according to graphs.
E: For Wings Front and Backing, cut two (one for Front and one for Backing) according to graph.

STITCHING INSTRUCTIONS
NOTE: C pieces are not worked.

1: Using colors and stitches indicated, work pieces according to graphs; with med. garnet, overcast bottom edges of B.

2: For Bodice, with white, whipstitch indicated edges of A wrong sides together; with white for armholes and vy. lt. sky blue for neck area, overcast armhole and neck areas. For Skirt,

with matching colors, whipstitch B and C pieces together as indicated on graphs; omitting attachment area, overcast top edge. Glue ½" lace to wrong side of bottom edge of Skirt and 2" lace to wrong side of Skirt on top of ½" lace, leaving 1⅜" [3.5cm] of lace showing at bottom edge (see photo). Matching center of Bodice to center of Skirt Front, with baby pink, whipstitch pieces right sides together as indicated.

NOTES: Cut ½" [13mm] off bottom edge of cone. Twist chenille stems together as shown in photo on page 87, making sure opening fits over cone 2" [5.1cm] from top and glue in place; cut off end of each chenille stem to measure 1½" [3.8cm] from cone and glue one arm on each chenille stem.

3: Place dress on cone, carefully pulling arms through armholes of Bodice. Place head on top of cone; glue to secure. Glue neck edge of Bodice to head. Overlap C pieces to fit snugly on cone and glue to cone to secure. Glue back of Bodice to cone.

NOTE: Cut two 4½" [11.4cm] pieces of 5" lace.

4: For sleeves (make 2), sew short edges of lace together with a ½" [13mm] seam. Gather long straight edge until it measures about 1" [2.5cm] across; tack to secure. Place gathered edge inside armhole of Bodice around arms and glue to secure. Gather ¾" [19mm] along scalloped edge to fit tightly on wrist; tack to secure.

5: For overskirt, with dk. aquamarine, whipstitch D pieces wrong sides together as indicated; with vy. lt. aquamarine, overcast unfinished edges. Glue overskirt to back of Skirt as shown in photo.

NOTE: Cut burgundy ribbon into one 1 yd. [0.9m] and one ½ yd. [0.5m] piece.

6: Tie a knot in center of 1 yd. piece; glue knot to center back of Skirt, letting ends hang down at each side of Angel. Pull one end to each side of Angel; make three large loops on each side of overskirt as shown and glue loops to secure.

7: Wrap ⅜" gold ribbon around waist of Skirt;

tie into a double-looped bow at back, trimming ends as desired. Fold remaining length of burgundy ribbon over and glue fold on top of gold bow so ends hang down in back.

8: For Wings, with vy. lt. gray green, whipstitch Backing E to wrong side of Front E; center and glue right side of Wings to back of Angel (see photo) over knots in ribbons.

9: Shape ⅛" gold ribbon into a circle for halo and glue ends together; glue to Angel's head as shown. Glue one silk flower to each sleeve at wrist (see photo) and remaining flowers to Overskirt as shown or as desired.

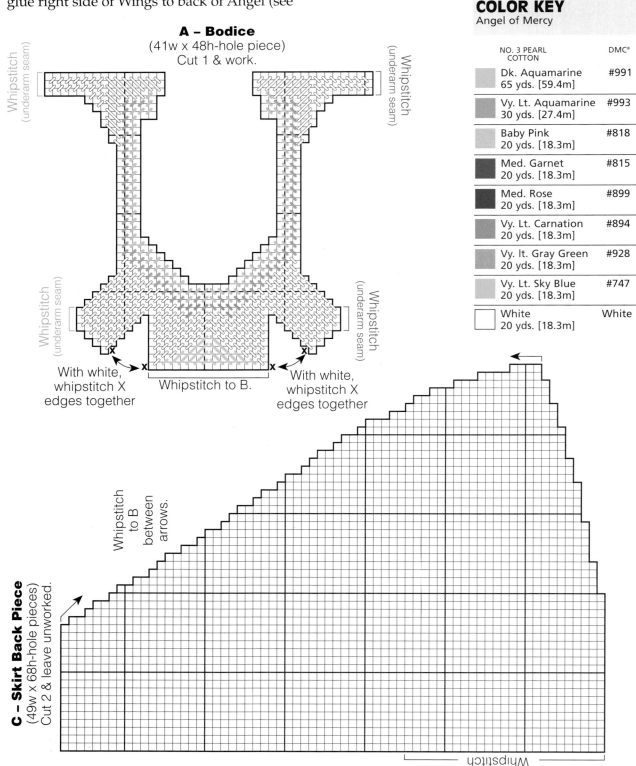

A – Bodice
(41w x 48h-hole piece)
Cut 1 & work.

Whipstitch (underarm seam)

Whipstitch (underarm seam)

Whipstitch (underarm seam)

Whipstitch (underarm seam)

With white, whipstitch X edges together

Whipstitch to B.

With white, whipstitch X edges together

Whipstitch to B between arrows.

C – Skirt Back Piece
(49w x 68h-hole pieces)
Cut 2 & leave unworked.

Whipstitch

COLOR KEY
Angel of Mercy

	NO. 3 PEARL COTTON	DMC®
	Dk. Aquamarine 65 yds. [59.4m]	#991
	Vy. Lt. Aquamarine 30 yds. [27.4m]	#993
	Baby Pink 20 yds. [18.3m]	#818
	Med. Garnet 20 yds. [18.3m]	#815
	Med. Rose 20 yds. [18.3m]	#899
	Vy. Lt. Carnation 20 yds. [18.3m]	#894
	Vy. lt. Gray Green 20 yds. [18.3m]	#928
	Vy. Lt. Sky Blue 20 yds. [18.3m]	#747
	White 20 yds. [18.3m]	White

B – Skirt Front

(92w x 68h-hole piece) Cut 1 & work.

Whipstitch to A.

Whipstitch to one C between arrows.

Whipstitch to one C between arrows.

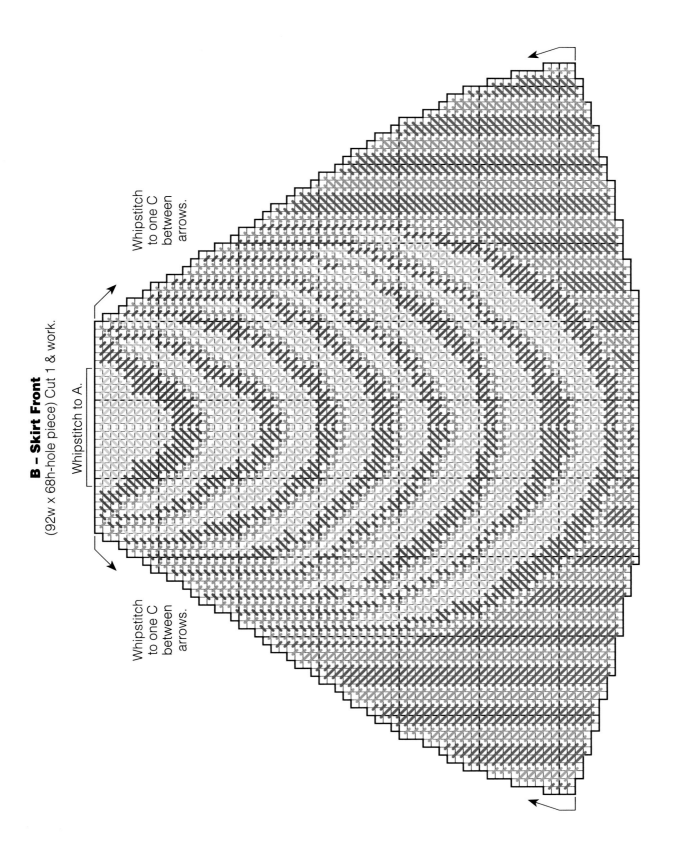

D – Overskirt Piece #1
(57w x 83h-hole piece)
Cut 1 & work.

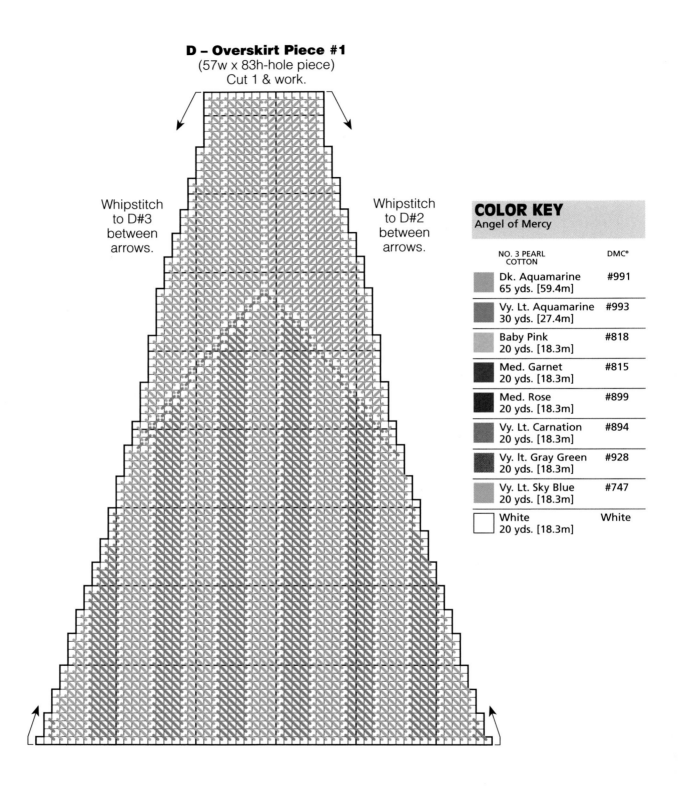

Whipstitch to D#3 between arrows.

Whipstitch to D#2 between arrows.

COLOR KEY
Angel of Mercy

NO. 3 PEARL COTTON		DMC®
	Dk. Aquamarine 65 yds. [59.4m]	#991
	Vy. Lt. Aquamarine 30 yds. [27.4m]	#993
	Baby Pink 20 yds. [18.3m]	#818
	Med. Garnet 20 yds. [18.3m]	#815
	Med. Rose 20 yds. [18.3m]	#899
	Vy. Lt. Carnation 20 yds. [18.3m]	#894
	Vy. lt. Gray Green 20 yds. [18.3m]	#928
	Vy. Lt. Sky Blue 20 yds. [18.3m]	#747
	White 20 yds. [18.3m]	White

D – Overskirt Piece #3
(63w x 84h-hole piece) Cut 1 & work.

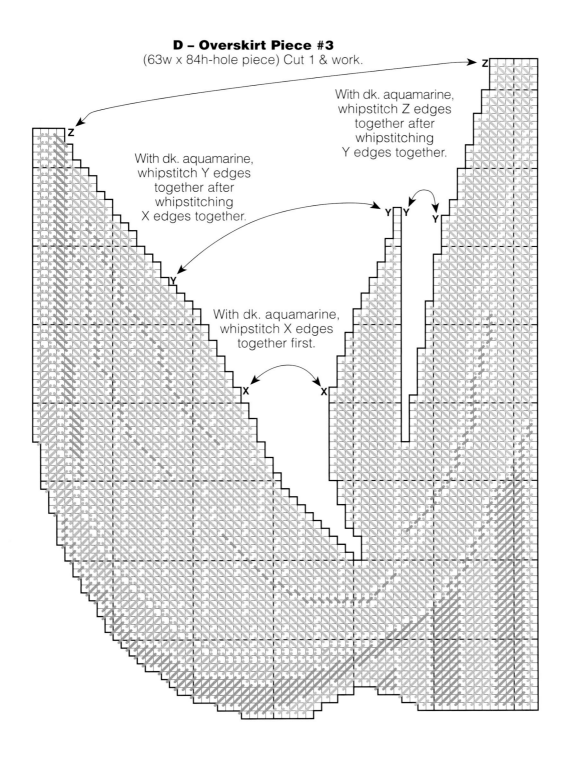

With dk. aquamarine, whipstitch Z edges together after whipstitching Y edges together.

With dk. aquamarine, whipstitch Y edges together after whipstitching X edges together.

With dk. aquamarine, whipstitch X edges together first.

D – Overskirt Piece #2
(63w x 84h-hole piece) Cut 1 & work.

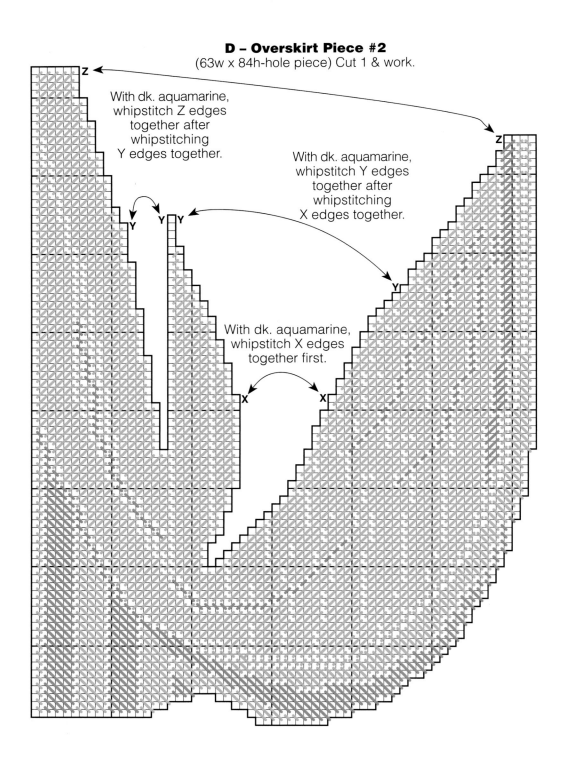

With dk. aquamarine, whipstitch Z edges together after whipstitching Y edges together.

With dk. aquamarine, whipstitch Y edges together after whipstitching X edges together.

With dk. aquamarine, whipstitch X edges together first.

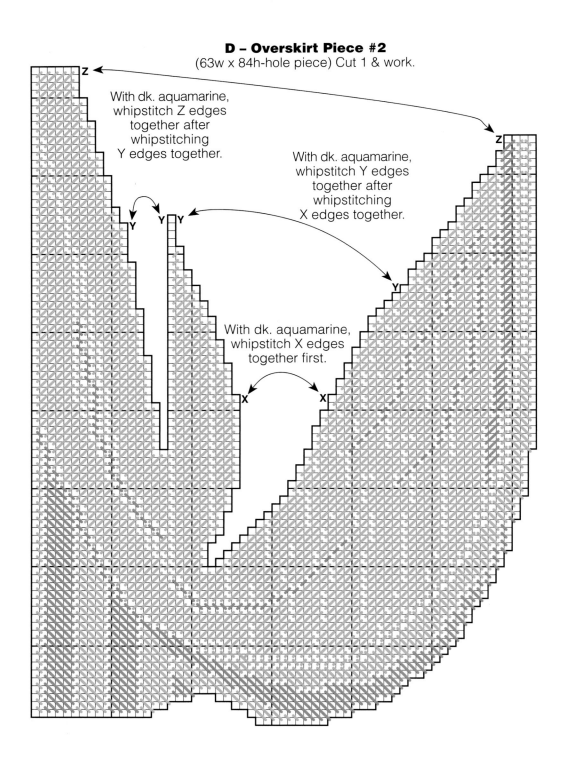

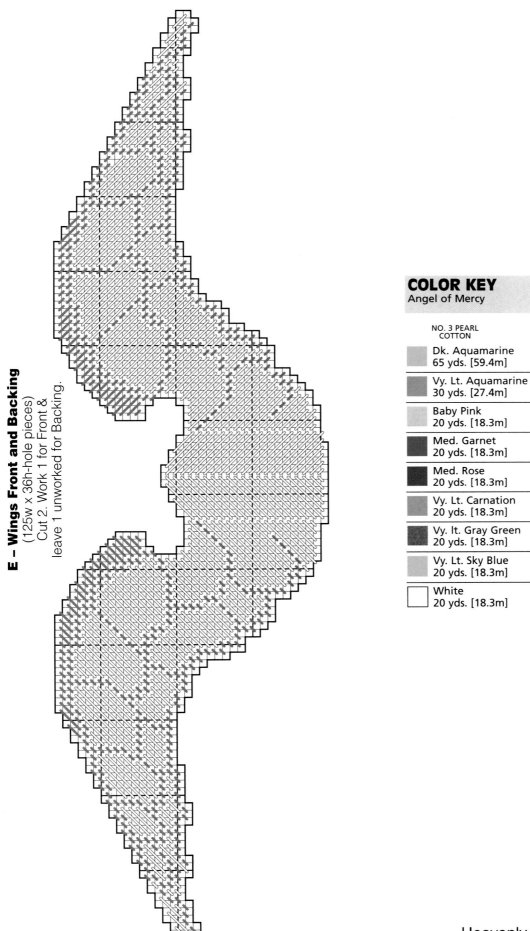

E – Wings Front and Backing
(125w x 36h-hole pieces)
Cut 2. Work 1 for Front &
leave 1 unworked for Backing.

Angel Portraits

Designed by Mike Vickery

SIZES
Portrait #1 is 11½" x 12⅝" [29.2cm x 32.1cm]
Portrait #2 is 10⅞" x 13½" [27.6cm x 33.5cm]

SKILL LEVEL
Easy

MATERIALS FOR ONE
• One 12" x 18" [30.5cm x 45.7cm] or larger sheet of 7-mesh plastic canvas
• Six-strand embroidery floss (for amounts see individual Color Keys on page 104)
• Worsted-weight or plastic canvas yarn (for amounts see individual Color Keys)

CUTTING INSTRUCTIONS
A: For Portrait #1, cut one 89w x 82h-holes.
B: For Portrait #2, cut one 77w x 95h-holes.

A – Portrait #1
(89w x 82h-hole piece)
Cut 1 & work, leaving uncoded areas unworked.

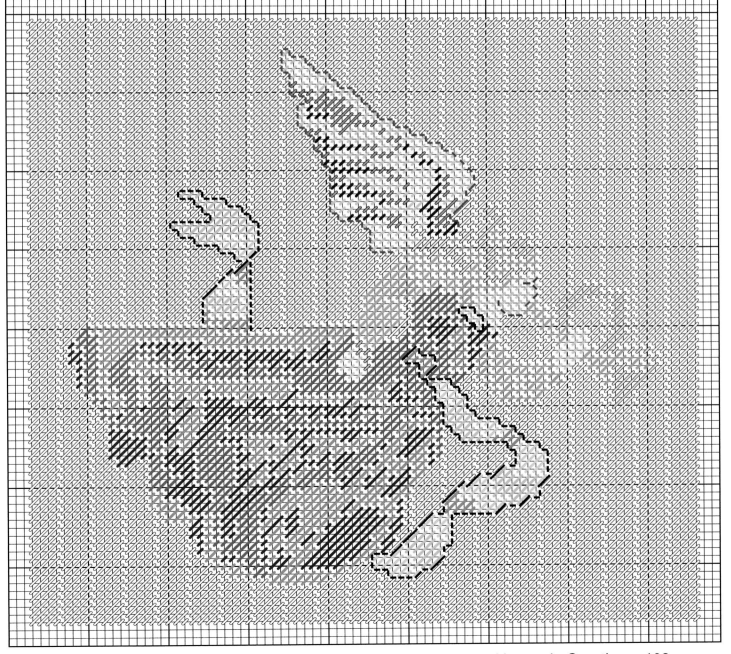

STITCHING INSTRUCTIONS

1: Using colors and stitches indicated, work Portrait according to graph of choice; do not overcast edges.

2: Using colors and embroidery stitches indicated, embroider detail on Portrait as indicated on graph. Frame as desired.

COLOR KEY
Portrait #1

EMBROIDERY FLOSS

■	Dk. Green 3 yds. [2.7m]
■	Lt. Gray 2 yds. [1.8m]
■	Lt. Brown ¼ yd. [0.2m]
■	Lt. Salmon ¼ yd. [0.2m]
■	Red ¼ yd. [0.2m]

WORSTED-WEIGHT

□	Eggshell 66 yds. [60.4m]
■	Red 9 yds. [8.2m]
■	Violet 9 yds. [8.2m]
■	Watermelon 9 yds. [8.2m]
■	White 3 yds. [2.7m]

WORSTED-WEIGHT

□	Yellow 3 yds. [2.7m]
■	Fern 2½ yds. [2.3m]
■	Holly 2½ yds. [2.3m]
■	Gold 2 yds. [1.8m]
■	Sail Blue 2 yds. [1.8m]
■	Silver 2 yds. [1.8m]
■	Baby Pink 1½ yds. [1.4m]
■	Gray 1½ yds. [1.4m]
■	Turquoise 1½ yds. [1.4m]
■	Forest 1 yd. [0.9m]
■	Pink ¼ yd. [0.2m]

COLOR KEY
Portrait #2

EMBROIDERY FLOSS

■	Gray 5 yds. [4.6m]
■	Red 5 yds. [4.6m]
■	Lt. Salmon 2 yds. [1.8m]
■	Turquoise 2 yds. [1.8m]
■	Lt. Brown ¼ yd. [0.2m]

WORSTED-WEIGHT

□	Eggshell 43 yds. [39.3m]
■	Yellow 10 yds. [9.1m]
■	Gold 9 yds. [8.2m]
■	Sail Blue 4 yds. [3.7m]

WORSTED-WEIGHT

■	Silver 4 yds. [3.7m]
■	White 4 yds. [3.7m]
■	Gray 3 yds. [2.7m]
■	Turquoise 3 yds. [2.7m]
■	Baby Blue 2½ yds. [2.3m]
■	Watermelon 2½ yds. [2.3m]
■	Baby Pink 2 yds. [1.8m]
■	Red 2 yds. [1.8m]
■	Violet 2 yds. [1.8m]
■	Pink 1 yd. [0.9m]

STITCH KEY

⊟ Backstitch/Straight

B – Portrait #2
(77w x 95h-hole piece)
Cut 1 & work, leaving uncoded areas unworked.

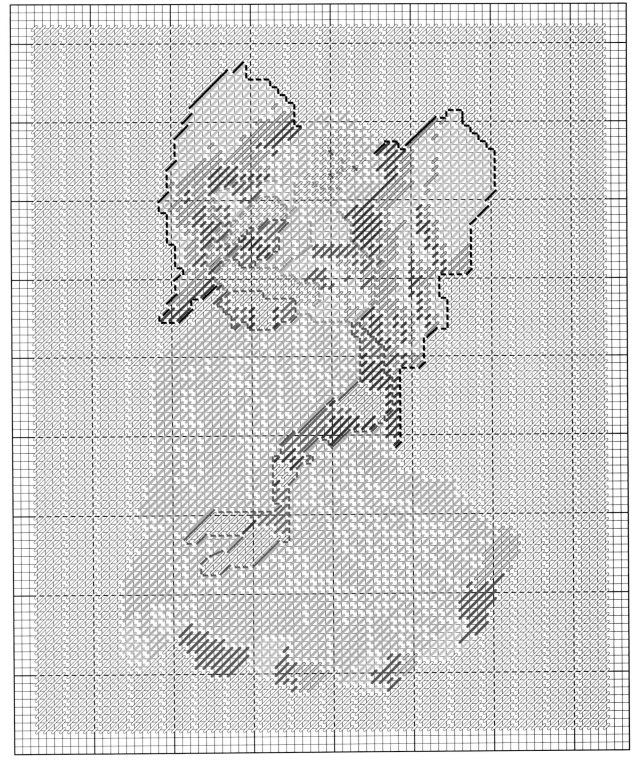

Pink Heart Lace Angel

Designed by Angie Arickx

SIZE
4" x 8⅜" x 10" tall [10.2cm x 21.3cm x 25.4cm]

SKILL LEVEL
Challenging

MATERIALS
- 1½ Sheets of 14-mesh Plastic Canvas by Darice®
- ½ Sheet of 10-mesh QuickCount® Plastic Canvas by Uniek Inc.
- One gold 3mm chenille stem
- One 3" [7.6cm] length of ³⁄₁₆" [5mm] wood dowel rod
- One 50mm Wood Doll Head With Drilled Center #1223-10 by Darice®
- Sunshine yellow curly doll hair
- One Pair 2½" [6.4cm] Plastic Hands #193292 by Crafts Etc.
- ⅓ yd. [0.3m] white ¼" [6mm] gold-trimmed ribbon
- Craft glue or glue gun
- ¹⁄₁₆" [2mm] Metallic Plastic Canvas Yarn by Rainbow Gallery® (for amount see Color Key)
- Six-strand Embroidery Floss Art. 117 by DMC® (for amounts see Color Key)

CUTTING INSTRUCTIONS
A: For Dress, cut one from 14-mesh according to graph.

B: For Sleeve Pieces #1 and #2, cut two each from 14-mesh according to graphs.

C: For Collar, cut two from 14-mesh according to graph.

D: For Wings, cut one from 10-mesh according to graph.

STITCHING INSTRUCTION
1: Using colors and stitches indicated, work pieces according to graphs; omitting attachment edges, with salmon for Dress and Sleeve Pieces, gold for Wings and with matching colors, overcast edges of pieces.

2: Using gold and backstitch, embroider detail on D as indicated on graph.

3: Fold Dress into a cone shape, overlapping straight edges one hole; glue to secure. For Sleeves (make 2), with salmon, whipstitch one B#1 and one B#2 wrong sides together; insert one hand into each Sleeve as shown in photo and glue to secure. With white, whipstitch C pieces wrong sides together.

4: Glue Sleeves to Dress so Collar will fit over top. Glue Collar in place over Sleeves (see photo).

5: Glue one end of dowel in doll head; glue desired amount of doll hair to head. Insert remaining end of dowel into opening on Collar and Dress; glue to secure.

6: Glue Wings to back of Angel (see photo). Make a 2" [5.1cm] circle in one end of chenille stem; bend and glue remaining end to center back of Wings so that circle rests on doll's head for a halo. Fold ribbon into a 1" [2.5cm]-wide bow; glue to Collar as shown.

B – Sleeve Piece #1
(50w x 37h-hole pieces) Cut 2 from 14-mesh & work.

Whipstitch to B#2.

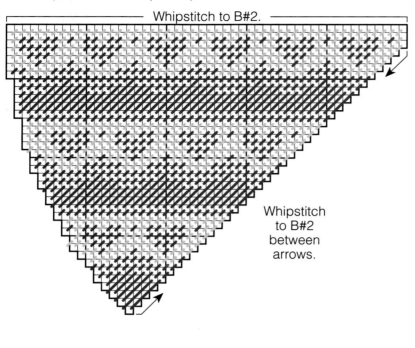

Whipstitch
to B#2
between
arrows.

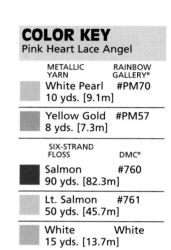

COLOR KEY
Pink Heart Lace Angel

METALLIC YARN	RAINBOW GALLERY®
White Pearl #PM70 10 yds. [9.1m]	
Yellow Gold #PM57 8 yds. [7.3m]	

SIX-STRAND FLOSS	DMC®
Salmon #760 90 yds. [82.3m]	
Lt. Salmon #761 50 yds. [45.7m]	
White White 15 yds. [13.7m]	

B – Sleeve Piece #2
(50w x 37h-hole pieces) Cut 2 from 14-mesh & work.

Whipstitch to B#1.

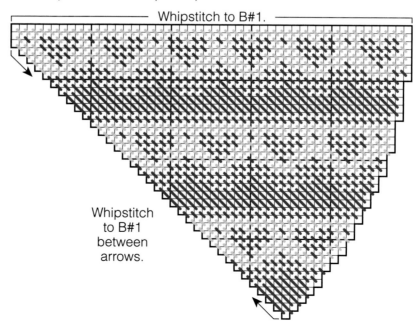

Whipstitch
to B#1
between
arrows.

D – Wings
(61w x 61h-hole piece)
Cut 1 from 10-mesh & work.

STITCH KEY
⊟ Backstitch

C – Collar
(30w x 30h-hole piece)
Cut 2 from 14-mesh & work.

Whipstitch

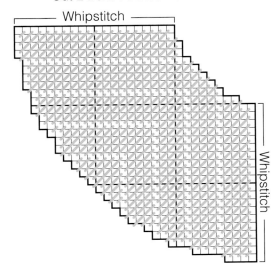

Whipstitch

A – Dress
(114w x 114h-hole piece) Cut 1 from 14-mesh & work.

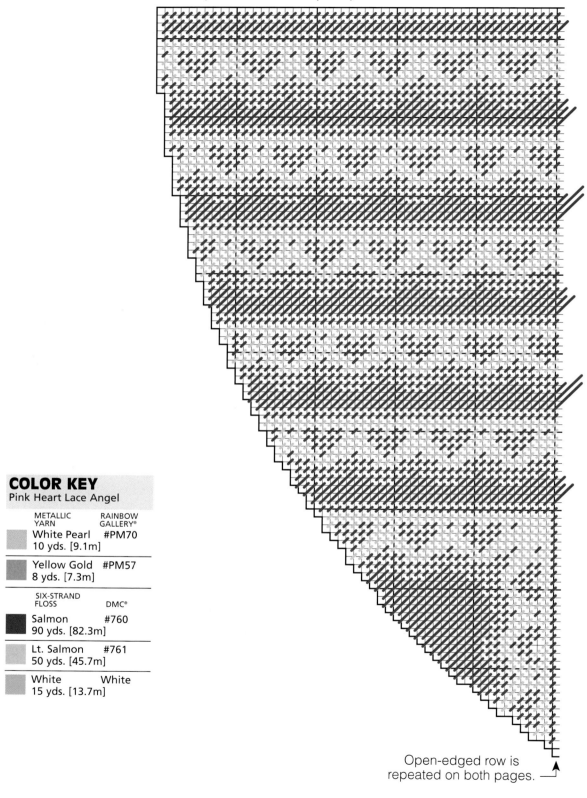

Open-edged row is
repeated on both pages.

COLOR KEY
Pink Heart Lace Angel

	METALLIC YARN	RAINBOW GALLERY®
	White Pearl 10 yds. [9.1m]	#PM70
	Yellow Gold 8 yds. [7.3m]	#PM57

	SIX-STRAND FLOSS	DMC®
	Salmon 90 yds. [82.3m]	#760
	Lt. Salmon 50 yds. [45.7m]	#761
	White 15 yds. [13.7m]	White

Pattern is
divided onto
two pages.

Open-edged
row is
repeated on
both pages.

Reflections of
Faith

When we walk to the edge of all the light we have and take that step into the darkness of the unknown, we must believe that one of two things will happen. There will be something solid for us to stand on or ... God will teach us how to fly!

Patrick Overton

Chapter Four

Holy City Tissue Cover

Designed by Joan Green

SIZE
Covers a boutique-style tissue box

SKILL LEVEL
Average

MATERIALS
• 1½ sheets of 10-mesh plastic canvas
• One dark sapphire 14 x 10mm oval cabochon
• Two dark sapphire 10 x 5mm navettes
• Craft glue or glue gun
• Plastic Canvas Metallic Yarn by Rainbow Gallery® or worsted yarn (for amounts see Color Key)
• No. 3 Pearl Cotton Art. 4583 by Anchor® (for amounts see Color Key)

CUTTING INSTRUCTIONS
A: For Top, cut one according to graph.

B: For Side #1, cut one according to graph.
C: For Sides #2, cut three 45w x 55h-holes.

STITCHING INSTRUCTIONS
1: Using colors and stitches indicated, work pieces according to graphs; omitting attachment edges, with desert lt., overcast cutout and edges of A.

2: Using copper and embroidery stitches indicated, embroider detail on B#1 as indicated on graph.

3: Using desert lt., whipstitch A and B pieces wrong sides together as indicated, forming Cover; overcast unfinished edges. Glue stones to Side #1 as indicated.

COLOR KEY
Holy City Tissue Cover

	METALLIC YARN	RAINBOW GALLERY®
	Gold 8 yds. [7.3m]	PM51
	Copper 4 yds. [3.7m]	PM53
	Peacock Blue 3 yds. [2.7m]	PM62

	NO. 3 PEARL COTTON	ANCHOR®
	Desert Med. 80 yds. [73.1m]	#373
	Desert Lt. 50 yds. [45.7m]	#372
	Fudge 17 yds. [15.5m]	#380
	Topaz Vy. Dk. 8 yds. [7.3m]	#310

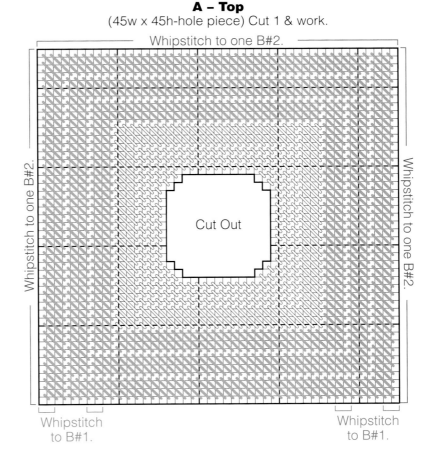

A – Top
(45w x 45h-hole piece) Cut 1 & work.

Whipstitch to one B#2.

Whipstitch to one B#2.

Whipstitch to one B#2.

Cut Out

Whipstitch to B#1.

Whipstitch to B#1.

B – Side #1
(45w x 70h-hole piece) Cut 1 & work.

Whipstitch
to A.

Whipstitch
to A.

STITCH KEY

— Backstitch/Straight
● French Knot

PLACEMENT KEY

☐ 14 x 10mm Dark
   Sapphire Oval
☐ 10 x 5mm Dark
   Sapphire Navette

COLOR KEY

Holy City Tissue Cover

METALLIC YARN	RAINBOW GALLERY®
Gold 8 yds. [7.3m]	PM51
Copper 4 yds. [3.7m]	PM53
Peacock Blue 3 yds. [2.7m]	PM62

NO. 3 PEARL COTTON	ANCHOR®
Desert Med. 80 yds. [73.1m]	#373
Desert Lt. 50 yds. [45.7m]	#372
Fudge 17 yds. [15.5m]	#380
Topaz Vy. Dk. 8 yds. [7.3m]	#310

C – Side #2
(45w x 55h-hole pieces) Cut 3 & work.

Whipstitch to A.

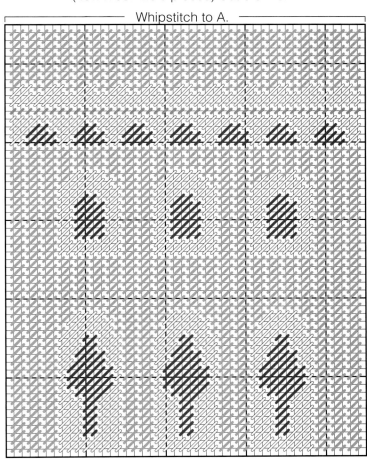

Star of David
Tissue Cover

Designed by Joan Green

SIZE
Loosely covers a boutique-style tissue box

SKILL LEVEL
Average

MATERIALS
- Two sheets of 7-mesh plastic canvas
- Twenty-one gold 4mm beads
- Sewing needle and gold thread
- Velcro® closure
- Craft glue or glue gun
- Plastic Canvas Metallic Yarn by Rainbow Gallery® or worsted yarn (for amounts see Color Key)
- Red Heart® Classic Art. E267 by Coats & Clark or worsted yarn (for amounts see Color Key)

CUTTING INSTRUCTIONS
A: For Top, cut one according to graph.
B: For Sides, cut four 31w x 37h-holes.
C: For Optional Bottom and Flap, cut one 31w x 31h-holes for Bottom and one 31w x 12h-holes for Flap (no graphs).
D: For Star, cut one according to graph.

STITCHING INSTRUCTIONS
NOTE: C pieces are not worked.

1: Using colors and stitches indicated, work A, B and D pieces according to graphs; with gold, overcast cutout edges of A and edges of D.

2: Using silver and straight stitch, embroider detail on A and D pieces as indicated on graphs. Using sewing needle and thread, attach beads to A and D pieces as indicated.

3: With silver, whipstitch A and B pieces wrong sides together, forming Cover. For Optional Bottom, with silver, whipstitch C pieces together and to one Cover Side according to Optional Bottom Assembly Illustration on page 120. Separate Velcro® closure; glue one side to Flap and one side to inside of corresponding Cover Side. Overcast unfinished edges of Cover. Glue Star to one Side as shown in photo.

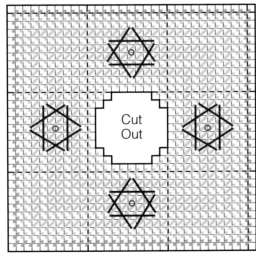

A – Top
(31w x 31h-hole piece) Cut 1 & work.

ATTACHMENT KEY
⊙ Bead

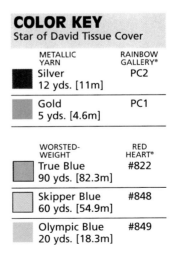

COLOR KEY
Star of David Tissue Cover

	METALLIC YARN	RAINBOW GALLERY®
■	Silver 12 yds. [11m]	PC2
■	Gold 5 yds. [4.6m]	PC1

	WORSTED-WEIGHT	RED HEART®
■	True Blue 90 yds. [82.3m]	#822
□	Skipper Blue 60 yds. [54.9m]	#848
▨	Olympic Blue 20 yds. [18.3m]	#849

STITCH KEY
− Straight

D – Star
(25w x 28h-hole piece)
Cut 1 & work.

B – Side
(31w x 37h-hole pieces) Cut 4 & work.

ATTACHMENT KEY

☐ Bead

STITCH KEY

⊟ Straight

Optional Bottom
Assembly Illustration

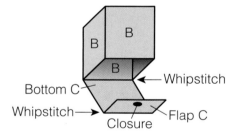

COLOR KEY
Star of David Tissue Cover

	METALLIC YARN	RAINBOW GALLERY®
	Silver 12 yds. [11m]	PC2
	Gold 5 yds. [4.6m]	PC1

	WORSTED-WEIGHT	RED HEART®
	True Blue 90 yds. [82.3m]	#822
	Skipper Blue 60 yds. [54.9m]	#848
	Olympic Blue 20 yds. [18.3m]	#849

Heavenly Triptych

Designed by Lee Lindeman

SIZE
½" x 12" x 11" tall [1.3cm x 30.5cm x 27.9cm]

SKILL LEVEL
Average

MATERIALS
- Two sheets of 7-mesh plastic canvas
- Two 9" x 12" [22.9cm x 30.5cm] sheets of black felt
- One 11" x 12" [27.9cm x 30.5cm] piece of ¼" [6mm] foam core board
- Craft glue or glue gun
- Six-strand Embroidery Floss Art. 117 by DMC® (for amount see Color Key)
- Needloft® Metallic Craft Cord by Uniek Inc. (for amount see Color Key)
- Needloft® Plastic Canvas Yarn by Uniek Inc. (for amounts see Color Key)

CUTTING INSTRUCTIONS
A: For Center Panel, cut one according to graph.
B: For Side Panels #1 and #2, cut one each according to graphs.

STITCHING INSTRUCTIONS
1: Using colors and stitches indicated, work pieces according to graphs; with black, overcast edges of pieces.

2: Using colors (Separate into individual plies if desired.) and embroidery stitches indicated, embroider detail on pieces as indicated on graphs.

B – Side Panel #2
(19w x 74h-hole piece)
Cut 1 & work, filling in uncoded areas using black & continental stitch.

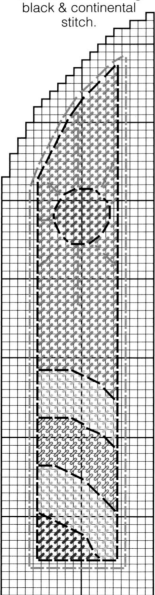

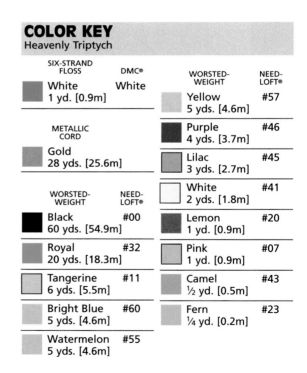

COLOR KEY
Heavenly Triptych

SIX-STRAND FLOSS	DMC®		
White 1 yd. [0.9m]	White		

		WORSTED-WEIGHT	NEED-LOFT®
		Yellow 5 yds. [4.6m]	#57
METALLIC CORD		Purple 4 yds. [3.7m]	#46
Gold 28 yds. [25.6m]		Lilac 3 yds. [2.7m]	#45
		White 2 yds. [1.8m]	#41
WORSTED-WEIGHT	**NEED-LOFT®**	Lemon 1 yd. [0.9m]	#20
Black 60 yds. [54.9m]	#00	Pink 1 yd. [0.9m]	#07
Royal 20 yds. [18.3m]	#32	Camel ½ yd. [0.5m]	#43
Tangerine 6 yds. [5.5m]	#11	Fern ¼ yd. [0.2m]	#23
Bright Blue 5 yds. [4.6m]	#60		
Watermelon 5 yds. [4.6m]	#55		

STITCH KEY

- Backstitch/Straight

NOTES: *Using pieces as a pattern, cut one each from foam core board. Using foam core board as a pattern, cut one each from felt 1" [2.5cm] larger at all edges. Cover each foam core board with corresponding felt piece, wrapping excess over edges and gluing to secure.*
For hinges, cut two 1½" x 8" [3.8cm x 20.3cm] pieces of felt.

3: Matching bottom edges and leaving a ³⁄₁₆" [5mm] space between pieces (see photo), glue one felt hinge to wrong side of A and B#1. Glue remaining felt hinge to wrong side of A and B#2. Glue wrong side of covered foam core board to wrong side of pieces.

A – Center Panel
(37w x 74h-hole piece)
Cut 1 & work, filling in uncoded
areas using black & continental stitch.

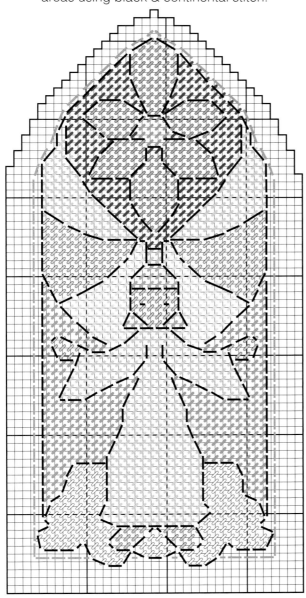

B – Side Panel #1
(19w x 74h-hole piece)
Cut 1 & work, filling in
uncoded areas using
black & continental
stitch.

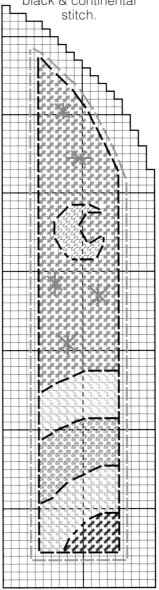

Shining Star

Designed by Terry Ricioli

SIZE
1" x 10¼" x 13½" tall [2.5cm x 26cm x 34.3cm]

SKILL LEVEL
Average

MATERIALS
•1½ sheets of 7-mesh plastic canvas
•Craft glue or glue gun
•Metallic Craft Cord by Darice® (for amount see Color Key)

CUTTING INSTRUCTIONS
   A: For Arm Piece #1, cut six according to graph.
   B: For Arm Piece #2, cut two according to graph.
   C: For Back Piece, cut one according to graph.

STITCHING INSTRUCTIONS
1: Using silver and stitches indicated, work pieces according to graphs; overcast edges of C.

2: Whipstitch A and B pieces wrong sides together as indicated and according to Star Assembly Illustration on page 126; overcast unfinished edges. Center and glue assembly to right side of C (see illustration). Display as desired.

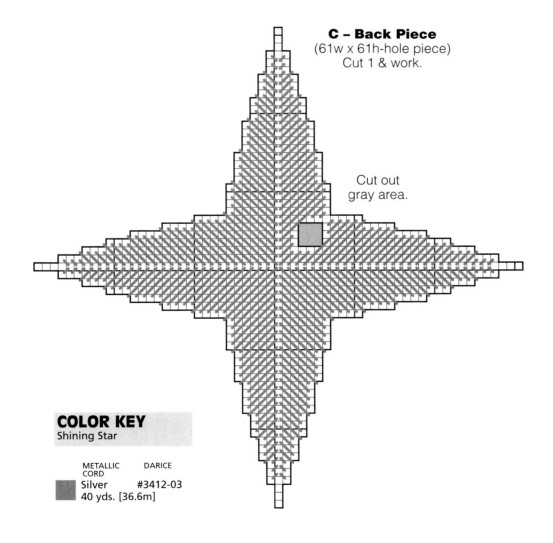

C – Back Piece
(61w x 61h-hole piece)
Cut 1 & work.

Cut out gray area.

COLOR KEY
Shining Star

	METALLIC CORD	DARICE
■	Silver 40 yds. [36.6m]	#3412-03

A – Arm Piece #1
(7w x 34h-hole pieces)
Cut 6. Work 3 &
3 reversed.

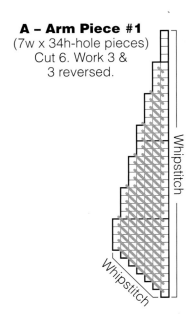

Whipstitch

Whipstitch

B – Arm Piece #2
(7w x 56h-hole pieces)
Cut 2. Work 1 &
1 reversed.

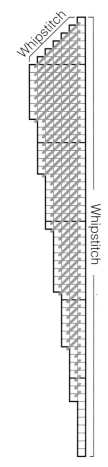

Whipstitch

Whipstitch

Star Assembly Illustration
(Pieces are shown in different
colors for contrast.)

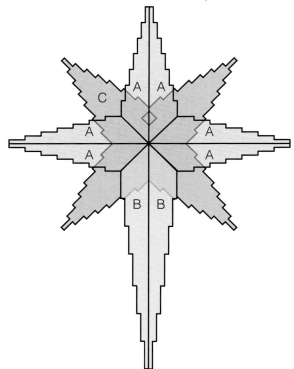

COLOR KEY
Shining Star

	METALLIC CORD	DARICE
	Silver 40 yds. [36.6m]	#3412-03

Folding Screen

Designed by Joan Green

SIZE
7½" x 11" [19cm x 27.9cm]

SKILL LEVEL
Average

MATERIALS
• One Sheet of 7-mesh Plastic Canvas by Darice®
• Plastic Canvas Metallic 7 Yarn by Rainbow Gallery® or worsted yarn (for amounts see Color Key)

CUTTING INSTRUCTIONS
For Screen Panels, cut three according to graph.

STITCHING INSTRUCTIONS
1: Using gold and continental stitch, work pieces according to graph; with indicated colors and as shown in photo, overcast cutouts.

2: With bronze, whipstitch pieces together as indicated on graph; overcast unfinished edges.

COLOR KEY		
Folding Screen		
METALLIC YARN	RAINBOW GALLERY®	
Gold 30 yds. [27.4m]	PC1	
Bronze 12 yds. [11m]	PC21	
Purple 8 yds. [7.3m]	PC15	
Blue 6 yds. [5.5m]	PC16	
Fuchsia 5 yds. [4.6m]	PC13	
Emerald Green 3 yds. [2.7m]	PC4	

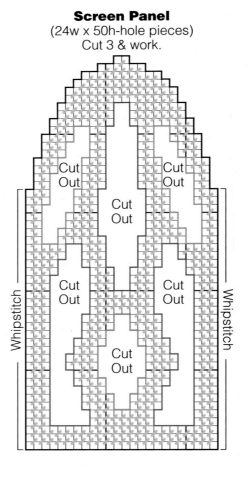

Screen Panel
(24w x 50h-hole pieces)
Cut 3 & work.

Stained Glass Window Bookend Cover

Designed by Joan Green

SIZE
Fits a 4⅝" x 5¼" x 5" tall [11.7cm x 13.3m x 12.7cm] metal bookend

SKILL LEVEL
Average

MATERIALS FOR ONE
• One Sheet of 7-mesh Plastic Canvas by Darice®
• One 6" x 9" [15.2cm x 22.9cm] piece of white felt
• Craft glue or glue gun
• Plastic Canvas Metallic Yarn by Rainbow Gallery® or worsted yarn (for amounts see Color Key)

CUTTING INSTRUCTIONS
For Bookend Cover Front and Back, cut two (one for Front and one for Back) according to graph.

STITCHING INSTRUCTIONS
NOTE: Back piece is not worked.

1: Using colors indicated and continental stitch, work Front according to graph; omitting attachment edges, with gold, overcast unfinished bottom edge.

NOTES: Using Back as a pattern, cut one from felt ⅛" [3mm] smaller at all edges.

2: Using gold PM51 and straight stitch, embroider detail on Front A as indicated on graph. With gold PC1, whipstitch Back to wrong side of Front as indicated. Glue felt to Cover Back.

COLOR KEY
Stained Glass Window Bookend Cover

	METALLIC YARN	RAINBOW GALLERY®
	Lt. Blue 12 yds. [11m]	PC14
	White Pearl 12 yds. [11m]	PC21
	Gold 10 yds. [9.1m]	PC1
	Gold 6 yds. [5.5m]	PM51
	Purple 5 yds. [4.6m]	PC15
	Fuchsia 2 yds. [1.8m]	PC13
	Emerald Green ½ yd. [0.5m]	PC4

STITCH KEY
—	Straight

Bookend Cover Front and Back
(36w x 57h-hole pieces)
Cut 2. Work 1 for Front, filling in uncoded areas using white pearl & continental stitch as shown in photo & leave 1 unworked for Back.

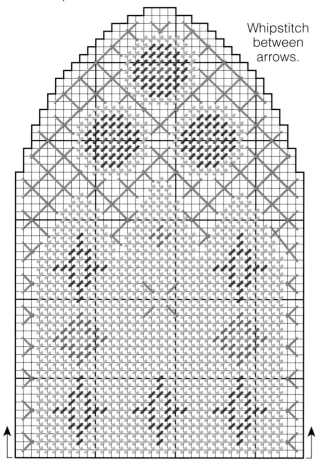

Whipstitch between arrows.

Celestial Bookmarks

Designed by Kristine Loffredo

SIZE
Each is about 2½" x 6" [6.4cm x 15.2cm]

SKILL LEVEL
Average

MATERIALS FOR ONE
- ½ Sheet of 7-mesh QuickCount® Plastic Canvas by Uniek Inc.
- #32 Metallic Braid by Kreinik Mfg. Co. (for amount see individual Color Key)
- Needloft® Plastic Canvas Yarn or worsted yarn (for amounts see individual Color Key)

CUTTING INSTRUCTIONS
A: For Dove Bookmark, cut one according to graph.

B: For Greek Cross Bookmark, cut one according to graph.

C: For Star Bookmark, cut one according to graph.

STITCHING INSTRUCTIONS
1: Using colors and stitches indicated, work Bookmark of choice according to graph; with matching colors and as shown in photo, overcast piece.

2: Using metallic braid and stitches indicated, embroider detail on piece as indicated on graph.

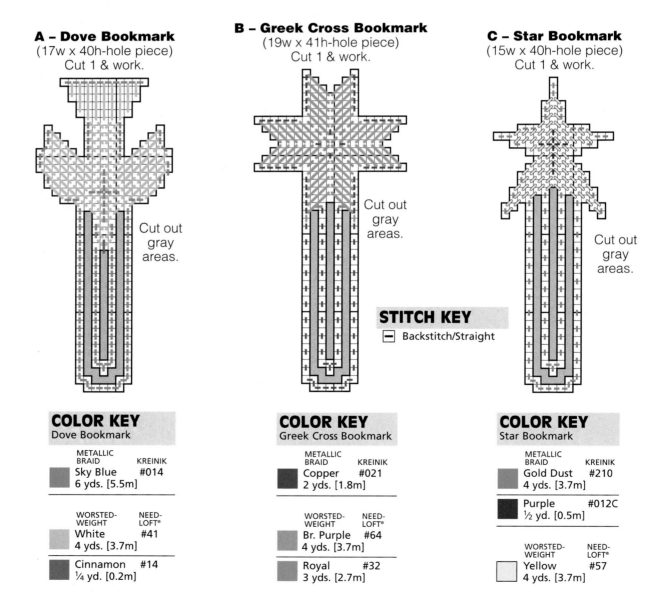

A – Dove Bookmark
(17w x 40h-hole piece)
Cut 1 & work.

Cut out gray areas.

B – Greek Cross Bookmark
(19w x 41h-hole piece)
Cut 1 & work.

Cut out gray areas.

C – Star Bookmark
(15w x 40h-hole piece)
Cut 1 & work.

Cut out gray areas.

STITCH KEY
- ▬ Backstitch/Straight

COLOR KEY
Dove Bookmark

METALLIC BRAID	KREINIK
Sky Blue 6 yds. [5.5m]	#014

WORSTED-WEIGHT	NEED-LOFT®
White 4 yds. [3.7m]	#41
Cinnamon ¼ yd. [0.2m]	#14

COLOR KEY
Greek Cross Bookmark

METALLIC BRAID	KREINIK
Copper 2 yds. [1.8m]	#021

WORSTED-WEIGHT	NEED-LOFT®
Br. Purple 4 yds. [3.7m]	#64
Royal 3 yds. [2.7m]	#32

COLOR KEY
Star Bookmark

METALLIC BRAID	KREINIK
Gold Dust 4 yds. [3.7m]	#210
Purple ½ yd. [0.5m]	#012C

WORSTED-WEIGHT	NEED-LOFT®
Yellow 4 yds. [3.7m]	#57

Silhouette Ornaments

Designed by Mike Vickery

SIZE
Each is 4¼" x 4¼" [10.8cm x 10.8cm]

SKILL LEVEL
Easy

MATERIALS
• One sheet of 7-mesh plastic canvas
• Plastic canvas metallic yarn or
  worsted yarn (for amounts see Color Key)

CUTTING INSTRUCTIONS
   A: For Ornament #1, cut one according
to graph.
   B: For Ornament #2, cut one according
to graph.
   C: For Ornament #3, cut one according
to graph.
   D: For Ornament #4, cut one according
to graph.

STITCHING INSTRUCTIONS
1: Using colors indicated and continental
stitch, work pieces according to graphs; with
royal, overcast pieces.

2: Using white and straight stitch, embroider
detail on A and C pieces as indicated on
graphs. Hang as desired.

A – Ornament #1
(28w x 28h-hole piece)
Cut 1 & work, filling in uncoded areas
using royal & continental stitch.

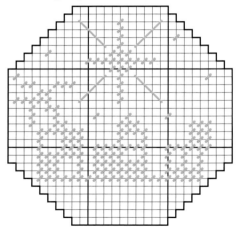

B – Ornament #2
(28w x 28h-hole piece)
Cut 1 & work, filling in uncoded areas
using royal & continental stitch.

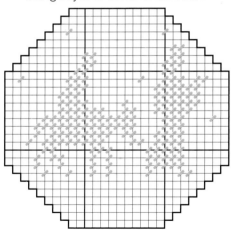

COLOR KEY
Silhouette Ornaments

	METALLIC YARN	
	Royal	40 yds. [36.6m]
	White	15 yds. [13.7m]

STITCH KEY
 Straight

C – Ornament #3
(28w x 28h-hole piece)
Cut 1 & work, filling in uncoded areas
using royal & continental stitch.

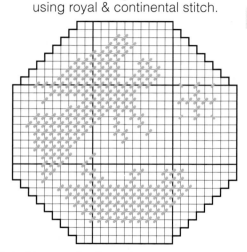

D – Ornament #4
(28w x 28h-hole piece)
Cut 1 & work, filling in uncoded areas
using royal & continental stitch.

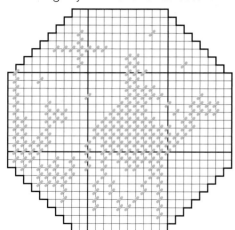

Menorah Tissue Cover

Designed by Mary Nell Wall

SIZE
Loosely covers a boutique-style tissue box

SKILL LEVEL
Average

MATERIALS
- Two sheets of 7-mesh plastic canvas
- Velcro® closure
- ⅛" [3mm] metallic ribbon or worsted yarn (for amount see Color Key)
- Red Heart® Classic Art. E300 by Coats & Clark or worsted yarn (for amounts see Color Key)

CUTTING INSTRUCTIONS
A: For Top, cut one according to graph.
B: For Sides #1 and #2, cut two each 31w x 37h-holes.
C: For Optional Bottom and Flap, cut one 31w x 31h-holes for Bottom and one 31w x 12h-holes for Flap (no graphs).

STITCHING INSTRUCTIONS
NOTE: C pieces are not worked.

1: Using colors and stitches indicated, work A and B pieces according to graphs.

2: Using gold and embroidery stitches indicated, embroider detail on A and B pieces as indicated on graphs.

3: Alternating Sides, with royal, whipstitch A and B pieces wrong sides together, forming Cover. For Optional Bottom, with royal, whipstitch C pieces together and to one Cover Side according to Optional Bottom Assembly Illustration. Separate Velcro® closure; glue one side to Flap and one side to inside of corresponding Cover Side. Overcast unfinished bottom edges of Cover.

A – Top
(31w x 31h-hole piece)
Cut 1 & work.

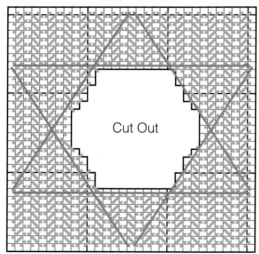

Optional Tissue Cover Bottom Assembly Illustration

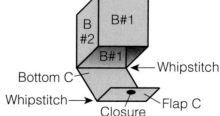

B – Side #1
(31w x 37h-hole pieces)
Cut 2 & work.

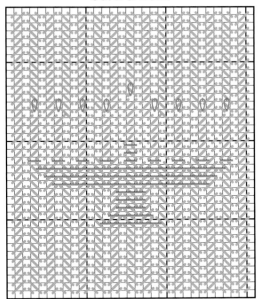

B – Side #2
(31w x 37h-hole pieces)
Cut 2 & work.

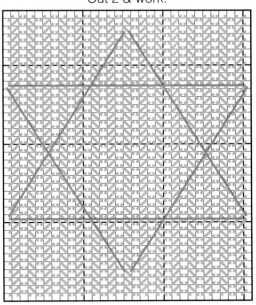

COLOR KEY
Menorah Tissue Cover

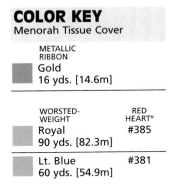

	METALLIC RIBBON	
	Gold 16 yds. [14.6m]	

	WORSTED-WEIGHT	RED HEART®
	Royal 90 yds. [82.3m]	#385
	Lt. Blue 60 yds. [54.9m]	#381

STITCH KEY

⊟ Straight
Lazy Daisy

Menorah Coasters & Box

Designed by Mary Nell Wall

SIZES
Each Coaster is 4¾" x 4¾" [12.1cm x 12.1cm];
Box is 5¼" x 5¼" x 1⅝" tall [13.3cm x
13.3cm x 4.1cm]

SKILL LEVEL
Average

MATERIALS
- Two sheets of 7-mesh plastic canvas
- ⅛" [3mm] metallic ribbon or worsted yarn
  (for amount see Color Key)
- Red Heart® Classic Art. E300 by Coats &
  Clark or worsted yarn (for amounts see
  Color Key)

CUTTING INSTRUCTIONS
  A: For Coasters, cut four 31w x 31h-holes.
  B: For Box Lid Top, cut one 35w x
35h-holes.
  C: For Box Lid Sides, cut four 35w x
4h-holes.
  D: For Box Sides, cut four 33w x 9h-holes.
  E: For Box Bottom, cut one 33w x 33h-holes
(no graph).

STITCHING INSTRUCTIONS
NOTE: E is not worked.
1: Using colors and stitches indicated, work
A-D pieces according to graphs; with royal,
overcast edges of A pieces.

2: Using gold and embroidery stitches
indicated, embroider detail on A and B pieces
as indicated on graphs.

3: With royal, whipstitch B and C pieces
wrong sides together, forming Lid; overcast
unfinished edges. Whipstitch D and E
pieces together, forming Box; overcast
unfinished edges.

COLOR KEY
Menorah Coasters & Box

METALLIC RIBBON		
	Gold	
	16 yds. [14.6m]	

WORSTED-WEIGHT		RED HEART®
	Royal	#385
	3 oz [85.1g]	
	Lt. Blue	#381
	3 yds. [2.7m]	

STITCH KEY
⊟	Straight
⬭	Lazy Daisy

A – Coaster
(31w x 31h-hole pieces)
Cut 4 & work.

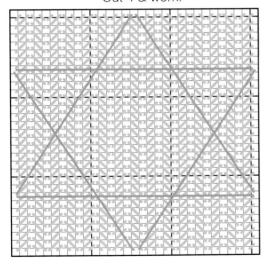

B – Box Lid Top
(35w x 35h-hole piece) Cut 1 & work.

D – Box Side
(33w x 9h-hole pieces) Cut 4 & work.

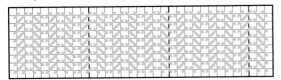

C – Box Lid Side
(35w x 4h-hole pieces) Cut 4 & work.

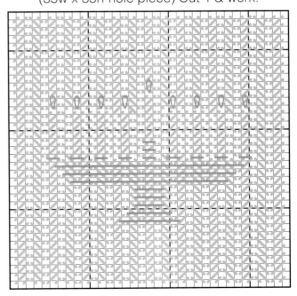

Scripture Sampler

Designed by Carole Rodgers

SIZE
13¾" x 16½" [34.9cm x 41.9cm], including Corner Motifs

SKILL LEVEL
Easy

MATERIALS
• Two sheets of 7-mesh plastic canvas
• Craft glue or glue gun
• Worsted-weight or plastic canvas yarn (for amounts see Color Key)

CUTTING INSTRUCTIONS
   A: For Picture, use one 90w x 70h-hole sheet.

   B: For Frame Pieces #1 and #2, cut two 90w x 5h-holes for #1 and two 5w x 80h-holes for #2 (no graphs).

   C: For Corner Motifs, cut four according to graph.

STITCHING INSTRUCTIONS
1: Using colors and stitches indicated, work A and C pieces according to graphs; using mid brown and long stitch over four bars, work B pieces. With matching colors, overcast edges of C pieces.

2: Using black (Separate into individual plies, if desired.) and embroidery stitches indicated, embroider detail on A as indicated on graph.

3: With mid brown, whipstitch A and B pieces together according to Frame Assembly Diagram. Glue Corner Motifs to Frame as shown. Hang as desired.

Frame Assembly Diagram
(Pieces are shown in different colors for contrast.)

Step 1:
Whipstitch one long edge of one B#1 to each long edge of A.

Step 2:
Whipstitch one long edge of one B#2 to one short edge of A & to short edges of adjacent B#1 pieces.

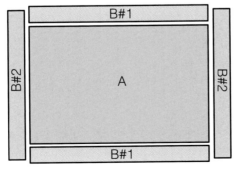

Step 3:
Overcast unfinished edges of B pieces.

A – Picture

Use one 90w x 70h-hole sheet & work.

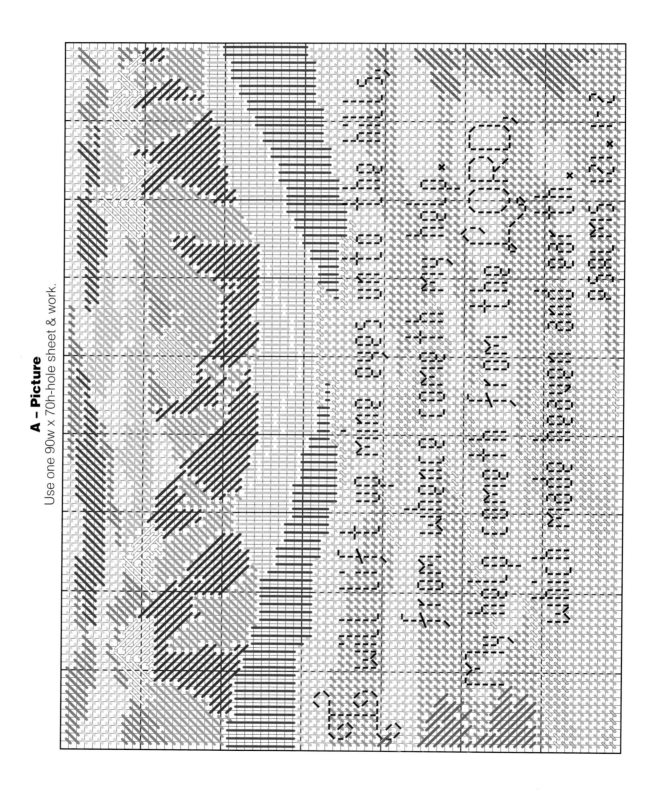

C – Corner Motif
(21w x 21h-hole pieces)
Cut 4 & work.

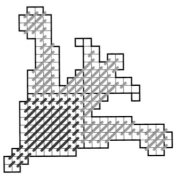

COLOR KEY
Scripture Sampler

	WORSTED-WEIGHT		WORSTED-WEIGHT
	Mid Brown 30 yds. [27.4m]		Olympic Blue 7 yds. [6.4m]
	Med. Sage 27 yds. [24.7m]		True Blue 7 yds. [6.4m]
	Lt. Sage 23 yds. [21m]		Nickel 6 yds. [5.5m]
	Blue Jewel 14 yds. [12.8m]		Forest 4 yds. [3.7m]
	Warm Brown 14 yds. [12.8m]		Med. Coral 4 yds. [3.7m]
	Purple 12 yds. [11m]		Sea Coral 4 yds. [3.7m]
	Lt. Plum 10 yds. [9.1m]		Tan 4 yds. [3.7m]
	Black 9 yds. [8.2m]		White 3 yds. [2.7m]
	Silver 9 yds. [8.2m]		Yellow 1 yd. [0.9m]
	Sky Blue 9 yds. [8.2m]		

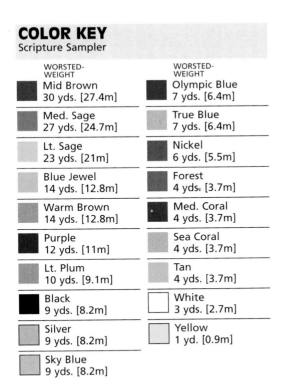

STITCH KEY

□ Backstitch/Straight

Nativity Screen

Designed by Sandra Miller Maxfield

SIZE
14½" x 21" [36.8cm x 53.3cm]

SKILL LEVEL
Average

MATERIALS
• 2½ sheets of 7-mesh plastic canvas
• Craft glue or glue gun
• Worsted-weight or plastic canvas yarn
  (for amounts see Color Key)

CUTTING INSTRUCTIONS
   A: For Center Panel, cut one according
to graph.
   B: For Side Panels #1 and #2, cut one each
according to graphs.
   C: For Star, cut one according to graph.

STITCHING INSTRUCTIONS
1: Using colors and stitches indicated,
work pieces according to graphs; omitting
attachment edges, with gold for Star and
with matching colors, overcast cutout on A
and edges of A-C pieces.

2: Using colors (Separate into individual
plies, if desired.) and embroidery stitches
indicated, embroider detail on A and B pieces
as indicated on graphs.

3: With mid brown, whipstitch A and B pieces
together as indicated on graphs. Glue Star
to Center Panel as shown in photo. Display
as desired.

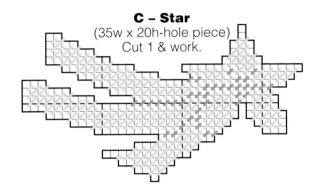

C – Star
(35w x 20h-hole piece)
Cut 1 & work.

COLOR KEY
Nativity Screen

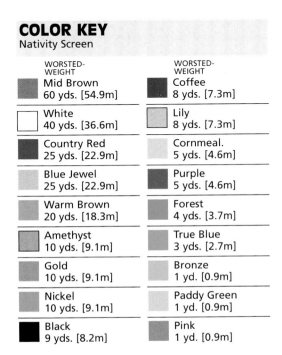

	WORSTED-WEIGHT		WORSTED-WEIGHT
	Mid Brown 60 yds. [54.9m]		Coffee 8 yds. [7.3m]
	White 40 yds. [36.6m]		Lily 8 yds. [7.3m]
	Country Red 25 yds. [22.9m]		Cornmeal. 5 yds. [4.6m]
	Blue Jewel 25 yds. [22.9m]		Purple 5 yds. [4.6m]
	Warm Brown 20 yds. [18.3m]		Forest 4 yds. [3.7m]
	Amethyst 10 yds. [9.1m]		True Blue 3 yds. [2.7m]
	Gold 10 yds. [9.1m]		Bronze 1 yd. [0.9m]
	Nickel 10 yds. [9.1m]		Paddy Green 1 yd. [0.9m]
	Black 9 yds. [8.2m]		Pink 1 yd. [0.9m]

STITCH KEY
⊟ Backstitch/Straight
⊡ French Knot

A – Center Panel
(70w x 90h-hole piece) Cut 1 & work.

Cut Out

Whipstitch to B#1.

Whipstitch to B#2.

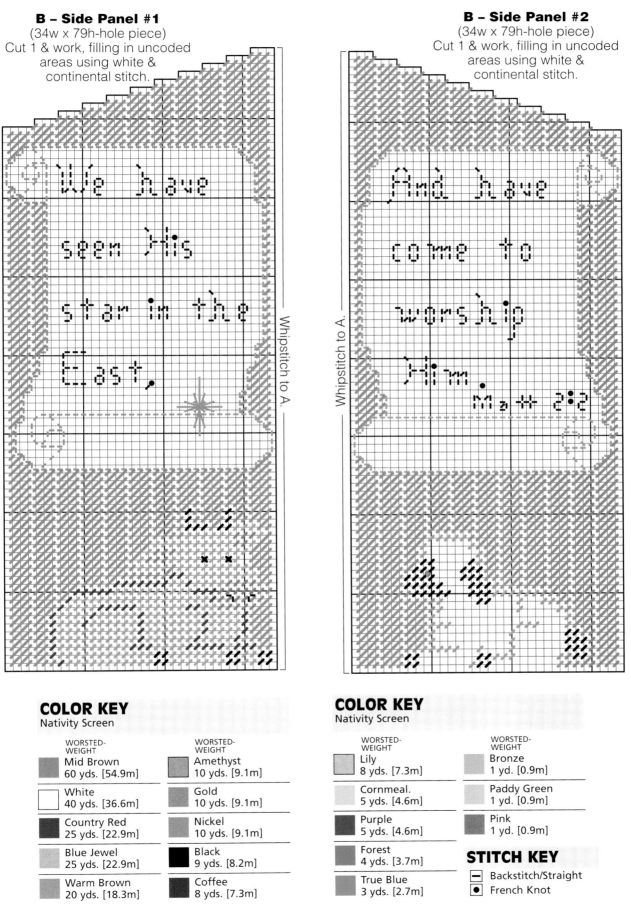

B – Side Panel #1
(34w x 79h-hole piece)
Cut 1 & work, filling in uncoded areas using white & continental stitch.

Whipstitch to A.

B – Side Panel #2
(34w x 79h-hole piece)
Cut 1 & work, filling in uncoded areas using white & continental stitch.

Whipstitch to A.

COLOR KEY
Nativity Screen

WORSTED-WEIGHT	
Mid Brown 60 yds. [54.9m]	Amethyst 10 yds. [9.1m]
White 40 yds. [36.6m]	Gold 10 yds. [9.1m]
Country Red 25 yds. [22.9m]	Nickel 10 yds. [9.1m]
Blue Jewel 25 yds. [22.9m]	Black 9 yds. [8.2m]
Warm Brown 20 yds. [18.3m]	Coffee 8 yds. [7.3m]

COLOR KEY
Nativity Screen

WORSTED-WEIGHT	
Lily 8 yds. [7.3m]	Bronze 1 yd. [0.9m]
Cornmeal. 5 yds. [4.6m]	Paddy Green 1 yd. [0.9m]
Purple 5 yds. [4.6m]	Pink 1 yd. [0.9m]
Forest 4 yds. [3.7m]	
True Blue 3 yds. [2.7m]	

STITCH KEY
— Backstitch/Straight
● French Knot

Nativity Ornaments

Designed by Sandra Miller Maxfield

SIZE
Each is about 3" x 5" [7.6cm x 12.7cm]

SKILL LEVEL
Average

MATERIALS
• Two sheets of 7-mesh plastic canvas
• Craft glue or glue gun
• Metallic cord (for amount see Color Key)
• Worsted-weight or plastic canvas yarn
 (for amounts see Color Key)

CUTTING INSTRUCTIONS
A: For Mary's Body, Mary's Arms and Mary's Hair, cut one each according to graphs.

B: For Joseph's Body, Joseph's Arm #1 and Joseph's Arm #2, cut one each according to graphs; for Mustaches, cut four according to graph.

C: For Baby Jesus' Manger, Baby Jesus' Body and Baby Jesus' Head, cut one each according to graphs.

D: For Wise Man #1 Body, Wise Man #1 Arms and Wise Man #1 Crown, cut one each according to graphs.

E: For Wise Man #2 Body, Wise Man #2 Arms and Wise Man #2 Crown, cut one each according to graphs.

F: For Wise Man #3 Body, Wise Man #3 Arms and Wise Man #3 Crown, cut one each according to graphs.

G: For Angel's Body and Angel's Wings, cut one each according to graphs.

H: For Donkey's Body, Donkey's Head and Donkey's Tail, cut two Bodies, one Head and one Tail according to graphs.

I: For Cow's Body, Cow's Head and Cow's Tail, cut two Bodies, one Head and one Tail according to graphs.

STITCHING INSTRUCTIONS
1: Using colors and stitches indicated, work pieces according to graphs; with matching colors as shown in photo, overcast edges of pieces.

2: Using colors (Separate into individual plies, if desired.) and embroidery stitches (See modified turkey work stitch illustration on page 159; leave ¼" [6mm] loops) indicated, embroider detail on Body A, Body B, Head C, Body D, Body E, Body F, Body G, Head H and Head I pieces as indicated on graphs.

NOTES: Cut one 9" [22.9cm] length of red yarn and one 3" [7.6cm] length of gold cord.
Cut one 3" [7.6cm] length each of green and warm brown yarn.

3: Tie red yarn into a bow; glue bow to right side of Angel's Body. For Angel's halo, shape cord into a circle; glue to wrong side of Angel's Body (see photo). For Joseph's headband, holding green and warm brown yarn together as one, tie a knot in one end and glue to wrong side of Joseph's Body. Twist strands together; tie a knot in remaining end and glue to wrong side of Joseph's Body (see photo).

4: For each Ornament, glue corresponding pieces together as shown. Hang as desired.

A – Mary's Arms
(13w x 10h-hole piece)
Cut 1 & work.

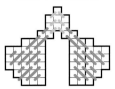

A – Mary's Body
(17w x 30h-hole piece)
Cut 1 & work.

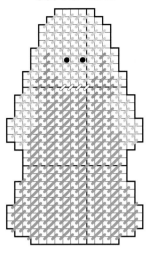

A – Mary's Hair
(8w x 5h-hole piece)
Cut 1 & work.

B – Joseph's Arm #1
(9w x 22h-hole piece)
Cut 1 & work.

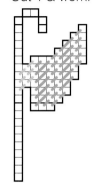

C – Baby Jesus' Manger
(22w x 22h-hole piece)
Cut 1 & work.

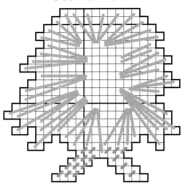

C – Baby Jesus' Body
(10w x 17h-hole piece)
Cut 1 & work.

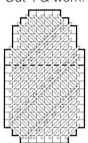

B – Joseph's Arm #2
(10w x 11h-hole piece)
Cut 1 & work.

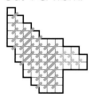

C – Baby Jesus' Head
(5w x 6h-hole piece)
Cut 1 & work.

B – Joseph's Body
(19w x 31h-hole piece)
Cut 1 & work.

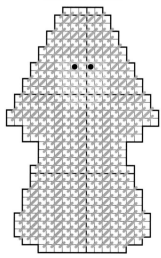

D – Wise Man #1 Body
(17w x 37h-hole piece)
Cut 1 & work.

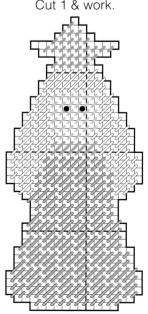

D – Wise Man #1 Arms
(15w x 12h-hole piece)
Cut 1 & work.

D – Wise Man #1 Crown
(7w x 7h-hole piece)
Cut 1 & work.

E – Wise Man #2 Body
(19w x 34h-hole piece)
Cut 1 & work.

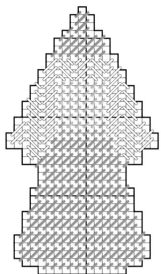

E – Wise Man #2 Crown
(7w x 7h-hole piece)
Cut 1 & work.

E – Wise Man #2 Arms
(15w x 14h-hole piece)
Cut 1 & work.

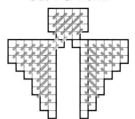

B – Mustache
(7w x 3h-hole piece)
Cut 4. Work 1 for Joseph,
1 for Wise Man #1,
1 for Wise Man #2 and 1
for Wise Man #3.

F – Wise Man #3 Body
(17w x 33h-hole piece)
Cut 1 & work.

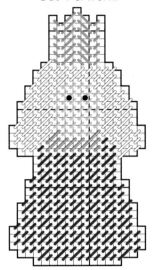

F – Wise Man #3 Crown
(7w x 7h-hole piece)
Cut 1 & work.

F – Wise Man #3 Arms
(15w x 11h-hole piece)
Cut 1 & work.

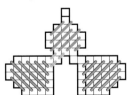

STITCH KEY

- − Backstitch/Straight
- ● French Knot
- ▲ Modified Turkey Work

COLOR KEY
Nativity Ornaments

METALLIC CORD	WORSTED-WEIGHT
Gold 6 yds. [5.5m]	Lily 8 yds. [7.3m]
WORSTED-WEIGHT	Parakeet 8 yds. [7.3m]
White 30 yds. [27.4m]	Mid Brown 7 yds. [6.4m]
Warm Brown 20 yds. [18.3m]	True Blue 7 yds. [6.4m]
Green 10 yds. [9.1m]	Black 6 yds. [5.5m]
Amethyst 8 yds. [7.3m]	Red 5 yds. [4.6m]
Blue Jewel 8 yds. [7.3m]	Cornmeal 2 yds. [1.8m]

G – Angel's Body
(17w x 30h-hole piece)
Cut 1 & work.

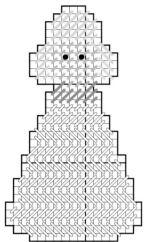

H – Donkey's Body
(13w x 15h-hole pieces)
Cut 2 & work.

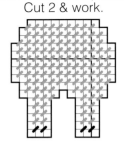

H – Donkey's Head
(9w x 16h-hole piece)
Cut 1 & work.

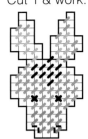

H – Donkey's Tail
(9w x 4h-hole piece)
Cut 1 & work.

G – Angel's Wings
(29w x 20h-hole piece)
Cut 1 & work.

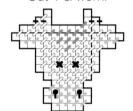

I – Cow's Head
(14w x 13h-hole piece)
Cut 1 & work.

I – Cow's Tail
(9w x 4h-hole piece)
Cut 1 & work.

I – Cow's Body
(13w x 18h-hole pieces)
Cut 2 & work.

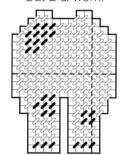

STITCH KEY

- – Backstitch/Straight
- • French Knot
- ▲ Modified Turkey Work

COLOR KEY
Nativity Ornaments

METALLIC CORD	WORSTED-WEIGHT
Gold 6 yds. [5.5m]	Lily 8 yds. [7.3m]
WORSTED-WEIGHT	Parakeet 8 yds. [7.3m]
White 30 yds. [27.4m]	Mid Brown 7 yds. [6.4m]
Warm Brown 20 yds. [18.3m]	True Blue 7 yds. [6.4m]
Green 10 yds. [9.1m]	Black 6 yds. [5.5m]
Amethyst 8 yds. [7.3m]	Red 5 yds. [4.6m]
Blue Jewel 8 yds. [7.3m]	Cornmeal 2 yds. [1.8m]

The Lion and the Lamb Coaster Set

Designed by Mary K. Perry

SIZES

Each Coaster is 3¾" x 3¾" [9.5cm x 9.5cm];
Holder is 1" x 4" x 2¼" tall [2.5cm x
10.2cm x 5.7cm]

SKILL LEVEL

Average

MATERIALS

• 1½ sheets of 10-mesh plastic canvas
• Sport-weight yarn (for amounts see
  Color Key)

CUTTING INSTRUCTIONS

A: For Coaster Fronts and Backs, cut four
each 37w x 37h-holes.

B: For Holder Front and Bottom, cut two
(one for Front and one for Bottom) 40w x
10h-holes.

C: For Holder Sides, cut two according
to graph.

D: For Holder Back, cut one 40w x
22h-holes.

STITCHING INSTRUCTIONS

1: Using colors and stitches indicated, work
pieces according to graphs.

2: Using colors (Separate into individual plies,
if desired.) and embroidery stitches indicated,
embroider detail on Front A pieces as indicated
on graph.

3: For Coasters (make 4), with dk. royal,
whipstitch one Front and one Back A piece
wrong sides together. Whipstitch B-D pieces
together as indicated, forming Holder; overcast
unfinished edges.

STITCH KEY

⊟ Backstitch/Straight

COLOR KEY
**The Lion and The Lamb
Coaster Set**

SPORT-
WEIGHT

■	Dk. Royal 2½ oz. [70.9g]
■	Black 12 yds. [11m]
■	Med. Brown 12 yds. [11m]
■	Tan 12 yds. [11m]
■	White 4 yds. [3.7m]
□	Off White 2 yds. [1.8m]

A – Coaster Front

(37w x 37h-hole pieces)
Cut 4 & work, filling in uncoded areas
using dk. royal & continental stitch.

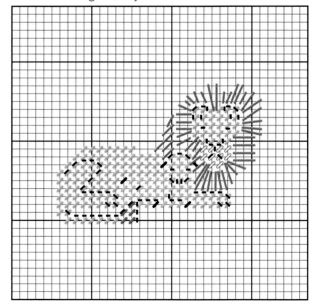

C – Holder Side

(10w x 22h-hole pieces)
Cut 2. Work 1 &
1 reversed.

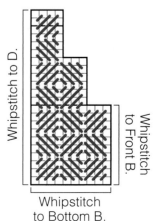

Whipstitch to D.

Whipstitch
to Front B.

Whipstitch
to Bottom B.

B – Holder Front and Bottom
(40w x 10h-hole pieces)
Cut 2; work 1 for Front & 1 for Bottom.

D – Holder Back
(40w x 22h-hole piece)
Cut 1 & work.

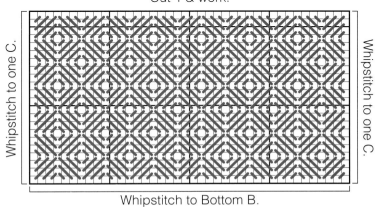

Whipstitch to one C.

Whipstitch to one C.

Whipstitch to Bottom B.

A – Coaster Back
(37w x 37h-hole pieces)
Cut 4 & work.

Ready, Set, Stitch

Get ready to stitch like a pro
with these simple, step-by-step guidelines.

GETTING STARTED

Most plastic canvas stitchers love getting their projects organized before they even step out the door in search of supplies. A few moments of careful planning can make the creation of your project even more fun.

First of all, prepare your work area. You will need a flat surface for cutting and assembly, and you will need a place to store your materials. Good lighting is essential, and a comfortable chair will make your stitching time even more enjoyable.

Do you plan to make one project, or will you be making several of the same item? A materials list appears at the beginning of each pattern. If you plan to make several of the same item, multiply your materials accordingly. Your shopping list is ready.

CHOOSING CANVAS

Most projects can be made using standard-size sheets of canvas. Standard-size sheets of 7-mesh (7 holes per inch) are always 70 x 90 holes and are about 10½" x 13½" [26.7cm x 34.3cm]. For larger projects, 7-mesh canvas also comes in 12" x 18" [30.5cm x 45.7cm],

which is always 80 x 120 holes and 13½" x 22½" [34.3cm x 57.2cm], which is always 90 x 150 holes. Other shapes are available in 7-mesh, including circles, diamonds, purse forms and ovals.

10-mesh canvas (10 holes per inch) comes only in standard-size sheets, which vary slightly depending on brand. They are 10½" x 13½" [26.7cm x 34.3cm], which is always 106 x 136 holes or 11" x 14" [27.9cm x 35.6cm], which is always 108 x 138 holes.

5-mesh canvas (5 holes per inch) and 14-mesh (14 holes per inch) sheets are also available.

Some canvas is soft and pliable, while other canvas is stiffer and more rigid. To prevent canvas from cracking during or after stitching, you'll want to choose pliable canvas for projects that require shap-

ing, like round baskets with curved handles. For easier shaping, warm canvas pieces with a blow-dry hair dryer to soften; dip in cool water to set. If your project is a box or an item that will stand alone, stiffer canvas is more suitable.

Both 7- and 10-mesh canvas sheets are available in a rainbow of colors. Most designs can be stitched on colored as well as clear canvas. When a pattern does not specify color in the materials list, you can assume clear canvas was used in the photographed model. If you'd like to stitch only a portion of the design, leaving a portion unstitched, use colored canvas to coordinate with yarn colors.

Buy the same brand of canvas for each entire project. Different brands of canvas may differ slightly in the distance between each bar.

MARKING & COUNTING TOOLS

To avoid wasting canvas, careful cutting of each piece is important. For some pieces with square corners, you might be comfortable cutting the canvas without marking it beforehand. But for pieces with lots of angles and cutouts, you may want to mark your canvas before cutting.

Always count before you mark and cut. To count holes on the graphs, look for the bolder lines showing each ten holes. These ten-count lines begin in the lower left-hand corner of each graph and are on the graph to make counting easier. To count holes on the canvas, you may use your tapestry needle, a toothpick or a plastic hair roller pick. Insert the needle or pick slightly in each hole as you count.

Most stitchers have tried a variety of marking tools and have settled on a favorite, which may be crayon, permanent marker, grease pencil or ball point pen. One of the best marking tools is a fine-point overhead projection marker, available at office supply stores. The ink is dark and easy to see and washes off completely with water. After cutting and before stitching, it's important to remove all marks so they won't stain yarn as you stitch or show through stitches later. Cloth and paper toweling removes grease pencil and crayon marks, as do fabric softener sheets that have already been used in your dryer.

CUTTING TOOLS

You may find it helpful to have several tools on hand for cutting canvas. When cutting long, straight sections, scissors, craft cutters or kitchen shears are the fastest and easiest to use. For cutting out detailed areas and trimming nubs, you may like using manicure scissors or nail clippers. If you prefer laying your canvas flat when cutting, try a craft knife and cutting surface—self-healing mats designed for sewing and kitchen cutting boards work well.

STITCHING MATERIALS

You may choose two-ply nylon plastic canvas yarn or four-ply worsted-weight yarn for stitching on 7-mesh canvas. There are about 42 yards per ounce of plastic canvas yarn and 50 yards per ounce of worsted-weight yarn.

Worsted-weight yarn is widely available and comes in wool, acrylic, cotton and blends. If you decide to use worsted-weight yarn, choose 100% acrylic for best coverage. Select worsted-weight yarn by color instead of the color names or numbers found in the Color Keys. Projects stitched with worsted-weight yarn often "fuzz" after use. "Fuzz" can be removed by shaving it off with a fabric shaver to make your project look new again.

Plastic canvas yarn comes in about 60 colors and is a favorite of many plastic canvas designers. These yarns "wear" well both while stitching and in the finished product. When buying plastic canvas yarn, shop using the color names or numbers found in the Color Keys, or select colors of your choice.

To cover 5-mesh canvas, use a doubled strand of worsted-weight or plastic canvas yarn.

Choose sport-weight yarn or #3 pearl cotton for stitching on 10-mesh canvas. To cover 10-mesh canvas using six-strand embroidery floss, use 12 strands held together. Single and double plies of yarn will also cover 10-mesh and can be used for embroidery or accent stitching worked over needlepoint stitches —simply separate worsted-weight yarn into 2-ply or plastic canvas yarn into 1-ply. Nylon plastic canvas yarn does not perform as well as knitting worsted when separated and can be frustrating to use, but it is possible. Just use short lengths, separate into single plies and twist each ply slightly.

Embroidery floss or #5 pearl cotton can also be used for embroidery, and each covers 14-mesh canvas well.

Metallic cord is a tightly-woven cord that comes in dozens of glittering colors. Some are solid-color metallics, including gold and silver, and some have colors interwoven with gold or silver threads. If your metallic cord has a white core, the core may be removed for super-easy stitching. To do so, cut a length of cord; grasp center core fibers with tweezers or fingertips and pull. Core slips out easily. Though the sparkly look of metallics will add much to your project, you may substitute contrasting colors of yarn.

Natural and synthetic raffia straw will cover 7-mesh canvas if flattened before stitching. Use short lengths to prevent splitting, and glue ends to prevent unraveling.

CUTTING CANVAS

Follow all Cutting Instructions, Notes and labels above graphs to cut canvas. Each piece is labeled with a letter of the alphabet. Square-sided pieces are cut according to hole count, and some may not have a graph.

Unlike sewing patterns, graphs are not designed to be used as actual patterns but rather as counting, cutting and stitching guides. Therefore, graphs may not be actual size. Count the holes on the graph (see Marking & Counting Tools), mark your canvas to match, then cut. The old carpenters' adage—"Measure twice, cut once"—is good advice. Trim off the nubs close to the bar, and trim all corners diagonally.

For large projects, as you cut each piece, it is a good idea to label it with its letter and name. Use sticky labels, or fasten scrap paper notes through the canvas with a twist tie or a quick stitch with a scrap of yarn. To stay organized, you many want to store corresponding pieces together in zip-close bags.

If you want to make several of a favorite design to give as gifts or sell at bazaars, make cutting canvas easier and faster by making a master pattern. From colored canvas, cut out one of each piece required. For duplicates, place the colored canvas on top of clear canvas and cut out. If needed, secure the canvas pieces together with paper fasteners, twist ties or yarn. By using this method, you only have to count from the graphs once.

If you accidentally cut or tear a bar or two on your canvas, don't worry! Boo-boos can usually be repaired in one of several ways: heat the tip of a metal skewer and melt the canvas back together; glue torn bars with a tiny drop of craft glue, super glue or hot glue; or reinforce the torn section with a separate piece of canvas placed at the back of your work. When reinforcing with extra canvas, stitch through both thicknesses.

SUPPLIES

Yarn, canvas, needles, cutters and most other supplies needed to complete the projects in this book are available at craft and needlework stores and through mail order catalogs. Other supplies are available at fabric, hardware and discount stores.

NEEDLES & OTHER STITCHING TOOLS

Blunt-end tapestry needles are used for stitching plastic canvas. Choose a No. 16 needle for stitching 5- and 7-mesh, a No. 18 for stitching 10-mesh and a No. 24 for stitching 14-mesh canvas. A small pair of embroidery scissors for snipping yarn is handy. Try using needle-nosed jewelry pliers for pulling the needle through several thicknesses of canvas and out of tight spots too small for your hand.

STITCHING THE CANVAS

Stitching Instructions for each section are found after the Cutting Instructions. First, refer to the illustrations of basic stitches found on page 159 to familiarize yourself with the stitches used. Illustrations will be found near the graphs for pieces worked using special stitches. Follow the numbers on the tiny graph beside the illustration to make each stitch—bring your needle up from the back of the work on odd numbers and down through the front of the work on the even numbers.

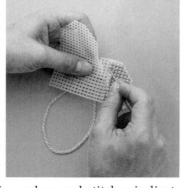

Before beginning, read the Stitching Instructions to get an overview of what you'll be doing. You'll find that some pieces are stitched using colors and stitches indicated on graphs, and for other pieces you will be given a color and stitch to use to cover the entire piece.

Cut yarn lengths between 18" [45.7cm] to 36" [91.4cm]. Thread needle; do not tie a knot in the end. Bring your needle up through the canvas from the back, leaving a short length of yarn on the wrong side of the canvas. As you begin to stitch, work over this short length of yarn. If you are beginning with Continental Stitches, leave a 1" [2.5cm] length, but if you are working longer stitches, leave a longer length.

In order for graph colors to contrast well, graph colors may not match yarn colors. For instance, a light yellow may be selected to represent the metallic cord color gold, or a light blue may represent white yarn.

When following a graph showing several colors, you may want to work all the stitches of one color at the same time. Some stitchers prefer to work with several colors at once by threading each on a separate needle and letting the yarn not being used hang on the wrong side of the work. Either way, remember that strands of yarn run across the wrong side of the work may show through the stitches from the front.

As you stitch, try to maintain an even tension on the yarn. Loose stitches will look uneven, and tight stitches will let the canvas show through. If your yarn twists as you work, you may want to let your needle and yarn hang and untwist occasionally.

When you end a section of stitching or finish a thread, weave the yarn through the back side of your last few stitches; then trim it off.

CONSTRUCTION & ASSEMBLY

After all pieces of an item needing assembly are stitched, you will find the order of assembly is listed in the Stitching Instructions and sometimes illustrated in Diagrams found with the graphs. For best results, join pieces in the order written. Refer to the Stitch Key and to the directives near the graphs for precise attachments.

FINISHING TIPS

To combat glue strings when using a hot glue gun, practice a swirling motion as you work. After placing the drop of glue on your work, lift the gun slightly and swirl to break the stream of glue, as if you were making an ice cream cone. Have a cup of water handy when gluing. For those times that you'll need to touch the glue, first dip your finger into the water just enough to dampen it. This will minimize the glue sticking to your finger, and it will cool and set the glue more quickly.

To attach beads, use a bit more glue to form a cup around the bead. If too much shows after drying, use a craft knife to trim off excess glue.

Scotchguard® or other fabric protectors may be used on your finished projects. However, avoid using a permanent marker if you plan to use a fabric protector, and be sure to remove all other markings before stitching. Fabric protectors can cause markings to bleed, staining yarn.

FOR MORE INFORMATION

Sometimes even the most experienced needle-crafters can find themselves having trouble following instructions. If you have difficulty completing your project, write to Plastic Canvas Editors, The Needlecraft Shop, 23 Old Pecan Road, Big Sandy, TX 75755, (903) 636-4000 or (800) 259-4000, NeedlecraftShop.com.

Stitch Guide

Continental

Modified Turkey Work

French Knot

Backstitch

Overcast

Lazy Daisy Stitch

Cross

Smyrna Cross
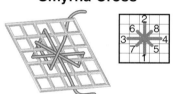

Mosiac

Straight
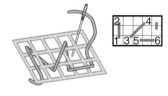

Whipstitch

Scotch Over Three Bars

Diagonal Horizontal
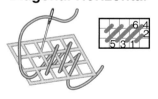

Bead Attachment
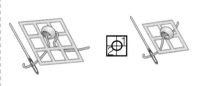

Reverse Scotch

Diagonal Vertical
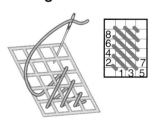

Diagonal Reverse Vertical
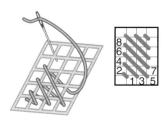

Alternate Scotch
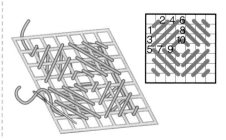

Pattern Index

Designer Index